The Matriarchs

A Novel by J.D. Fox

The Matriarchs
A Novel by J.D. Fox
Copyright © 2011 by J.D. Fox

FIRST EDITION
Printed in the United States
ISBN-13: 978-1456462291
ISBN-10: 1456462296

Cover and book design by Paula Doubleday Design Inc.

Dedication

To the women who made this
book possible . . . and necessary.

Pre-Law

"This is the first chance we've had to go shopping together," said Laura, who everyone else deferred to as the First Matriarch.

Saks Fifth Avenue, the original at the corner of 5th Avenue and 50th Street in Manhattan, catered to women like Laura and her chosen colleagues. Usually, the forty-something women visited their personal shopper individually, or just had her send recommended wardrobe additions to their homes to be tried on. Today, their busy schedules allowed a collective hour away from the office, and one of the firm's drivers was available too. It was just a 10-minute drive from their Times Square headquarters.

Susan from Saks, as they called her, was more than prepared for their impromptu group visit. In addition to her own office and client changing room, Susan commandeered the salons adjoining hers and the connecting conference room. Saks was always happy to accommodate successful clients who spent thousands of dollars on clothes. They'd even have the food service bring up a little something.

"As soon as the new Armani suits came in, I knew you'd have to see them, Ms. Henderson," said the motivated personal shopper.

"Susan, for the thousandth time, it's Laura," said the First Matriarch, running her hand along the lush fabric and finished interior seams. "But don't I already have a suit in this shade of grey?"

Susan knew her customers, and their purchase files, and was ready with a response: "You do have a similar shade, from four years ago. But the shoulders were cut a little differently that year than they are now. Since you wear suits every day, I think you'll get plenty of wear out of both."

Laura smiled like a teacher whose student had just passed an easy but important test. Her personal shopper knew what customers liked, made them look good, and would be worth the investment in this year's Armani. There was no need to actually try on the new suits. They would fit.

Mindy, Carol and Connie nodded their approval. Susan from Saks was their personal shopper too, introduced by Laura when each one, in turn, entered the Matriarchs' world – Mindy first, then Carol, then Connie.

It was easy enough to tell the women worked as a team, in addition to their polished professional wardrobes. They each proudly wore an expensive symbol of their membership in this exclusive club – large, rare, square-cut pale blue diamonds, mounted on platinum rings. Laura, Mindy, Carol and Connie wore those rings to work every day. No one else at their law firm, not even the impressively salaried female partners, had diamonds of this size, clarity, or obvious purpose. The rings signaled who was really in charge at the offices of Fishbein, Schindler, Rose and Sampson.

"I'm not the only one shopping today, am I?" Laura said with a smile. "What do we have for my colleagues?"

Mindy, Carol and Connie were instantly presented with designer jackets, skirts and blouses individually chosen to complement their figures. If there was time, Susan from Saks also had shoes and belts ready for inspection.

"Such lovely clothes," said Connie, who recruited new lawyers to the firm. "So much nicer than the interview suits I've been seeing on the law students for the past few months at job fairs."

"How does our new crop look?" said Laura, simultaneously trying to decide if one of the blouses on the table would be appropriate for the office.

"I think we're almost there," said Connie. "I've got most of the commitments nailed down, with just a couple of recruits to secure in the next few days."

"It would be nice if we could get them a little cheaper, especially since the market has been so volatile the past few years," said Carol, who was in charge of the finances. Carol winked at Connie. The cost of new associates was fully budgeted against current business, and they yielded a profit as soon as they walked in the door. It was just Carol's job to nag everyone about watching the pennies. And to always be prepared to downsize, or "right-size," if billings went down. And all those other clichés financial services people like to toss around.

Mindy, Laura's initial Matriarch recruit and trusted right hand, saw an opportunity to enter the conversation with a tactic emphasized at her evening business school classes – the compliment. "Connie, recruiting the top students from both the first- and second-tier law schools is brilliant. The first-tier students feel entitled to work with us, but always have to keep an eye on the hungry second tier. Healthy competition"

Laura nodded in agreement, and decided against the blouse. Too many frills.

"It would be nice if we could extend the motivation of our first year associates to our more senior attorneys," said Carol, which brought smiles from all four assembled Matriarchs.

"There are only two of them left," Laura said. Everyone knew she meant Albert Rose and Oscar Sampson, the two remaining founding partners of Fishbein, Schindler, Rose and Sampson. "The old boys won't last forever," she added.

"Ladies, do we have time for a look at the shoes?" asked Susan from Saks, hoping for a record sales day. She knew these customers knew shoes.

"I think we can spare a few more minutes," said Laura,

glancing quickly at her Cartier watch. "My next meeting isn't for another hour."

On cue, four racks appeared with the season's newest designer creations – or at least the low-heeled, sensible varieties that would hold up for a day at the Fishbein headquarters office without inflicting too much heel pain.

"These are beautiful," Mindy said, grabbing one of the shoes off her designated rack and turning it over to confirm her familiarity with the designer. Unlike the 8th floor shoe salon of Saks Fifth Avenue, which famously has its own New York City zip code (10022), there were no prices on the undersides of these shoes. On this rare group expedition, the Matriarchs weren't looking for bargains.

"Here's a terrific pair," said Carol, the firm's CFO. "But I think I'm already set for navy blue shoes."

"I thought it might be time to replace the pair you bought three years ago," said Susan from Saks.

"Or I could just get the ones I have re-heeled," Carol replied, the accountant in her looking for the cheapest possible option.

"Get them," said Laura. "Everyone deserves to treat themselves well, when they work as hard as we do."

Laura's mobile phone, which she had set next to her purse on the conference table, began to ring. Her assistant knew Laura was out for a rare outing with her Matriarchs, and would only call for an emergency.

"Yes, what is it?" Laura asked as soon as she picked up the phone.

"You need to come back to the office right away," said her assistant Toni, not even bothering to apologize for the interruption.

"What's the matter?"

"There's something wrong with Mr. Rose," Toni said. "His secretary just called 9-1-1 to get an ambulance."

Fishbein, Schindler, Rose and Sampson had just lost its third founding partner.

One

Sam Mitcham was about to win. He could feel it.

He was sitting in New York Family Court in a nondescript building in downtown Manhattan. To his left sat Jane Chapnick, his favorite professor and director of the Child Advocacy Clinic at Columbia, his Ivy League law school. To his right, their client, Michele King.

Michele had a child when she was 15, still a child herself. The father wasn't in court, and wasn't a part of this proceeding. It was all about Michele, and whether she had straightened out her life enough to be granted full custody of her four-year-old son.

Sam's role was to establish and maintain contact with Michele, research her case, draft all the Family Court paperwork, and sit through round after round of hearings. Establishing rapport with Michele was the easy part. She'd warmed to him immediately when he began calling her "One-L Michele."

The hard part was figuring out the legal strategy, and how to make the system work for Michele. For that, he had Jane Chapnick. She was the former attorney-in-charge of Mothers Need Lawyers, and now a Columbia Law School clinical professor. Chapnick had seen the ugly side of custody battles, and after 20 years, figured her most important contribution was to nurture the next generation of competent family advocates, students like Sam Mitcham.

"Full custody is granted," said the judge. Sam looked over at Michele. She wasn't crying. She wasn't even smiling. She just looked ready ... ready to assume the responsibility for the son she could now truly call her own.

After the hugs and congratulations between attorneys and client, Sam and Jane walked to the exit. He knew it would be hard to disappoint her after this victory, but he'd stalled long enough.

"So, tell me," Jane Chapnick said. "Ready to accept the job offer from Mothers Need Lawyers?" She'd made the introduction, coached him through each interview, and knew he'd be a perfect fit for the organization she founded. "You'll have lots of successes like the one we had today," she said. "We've given Michele the chance to become a real mom."

"I can't tell you how grateful I am for everything you've done, and everything you do every day," Sam said, deciding to lay it on a little thick. "I love Mothers Need Lawyers, and the idea of doing work that makes a difference."

"But?" asked his professor.

"But I don't love the idea of being a poor public interest lawyer in New York City."

Jane Chapnick had heard this before, many times, often from her brightest students. She could immediately tell his mind was made up, but had to make her own argument anyway ... yet again.

"You know your law school debt will be forgiven if you take this job," she said, not a question but a statement of fact.

"Yes, and that's a major consideration, but I'd still be living on a salary that would barely cover rent on a bad studio apartment." Doing "Blessed Work," as one of his cynical Columbia corporate law professors not in Jane Chapnick's camp put it, was certainly appealing. But who wants to spend their mid '20s in New York, one of the world's most expensive cities, with no money to spend?

"You have another offer, don't you?" said Professor Chapnick. "For a lot of money?"

"Yep," Sam said, suddenly sounding like the Midwesterner he was. "Fishbein, Schindler, Rose, and Sampson."

"The Big Fish," she said, nodding her head. She didn't have to ask other questions. If Sam was making this decision based on money, or even prestige, her argument was over.

Jane Chapnick was well acquainted with Fishbein, Schindler, Rose, and Sampson – one of the world's largest corporate law firms. Headquarters in New York's Times Square. Nine hundred lawyers in New York alone, another 600 in 20 offices around the world. Billions of dollars in revenue. Wherever big deals were happening, announced by *The Wall Street Journal* or *The Daily Deal*, Fishbein would be listed as counsel to one of the marrying or divorcing companies.

"You had a nice summer with them, didn't you?" Jane asked.

"Doesn't everyone?" Sam replied.

Fishbein, like all its peers, recruited top law school students to become summer associates, sort of an elaborate tryout to see if students had the right stuff to be offered real jobs upon graduation.

"Well, why wouldn't they want you?" the professor continued. "You're at the top of your class, everyone likes you, and you probably left the impression you want to spend the rest of your career in the world of corporate restructuring."

"I've been told that I took all the right courses, they were impressed with my grades, and I apparently interview well," he said, with a note of accomplishment.

Jane Chapnick saw one more chance to play the guilt card. "So, you spent the Fishbein summer like all the other associates – a little work, a lot of socializing. The menu included Broadway shows, cruises around New York's harbor, Yankees and Mets games, and concerts at Madison Square Garden. Fishbein always bought the best seats in the house, right?"

"They were very hospitable, yes," Sam said, looking at his shoes and hoping Jane would wrap this up sooner than later.

"Damn it, it's impossible to beat them at this game," she continued. "The wining and dining almost always work. You were impressed, and want more. And during the school term following your blissful summer, they started turning up the heat."

Over the course of his third year of law school, which was mostly spent with Jane Chapnick's Child Advocacy Clinic, Sam did keep in touch with Fishbein. Specifically, he kept in touch with Matriarch Connie.

Sam had heard about the Matriarchs over the summer, as tales of them were an essential part of Fishbein's lore. As powerful in their world as Jane Chapnick was in hers, they ran all the key functions of the billion-dollar firm – administration, finance, recruiting, and case management. They'd each been around more than 20 years, time enough to see Fishbein grow into an international powerhouse.

Matriarch Connie's official title was Director of Legal Recruiting. Sam knew Connie and the rest of the Matriarchs were quite different than the poor but deserving mother he just represented in court. They had access to financial resources – they were rich.

The offer Matriarch Connie made a week ago was top-dollar, enough to start paying off Sam's six-figure law school debt and live with some style in New York. "Of course, I'll also be able to provide the Fishbein seats to new Broadway shows once in awhile," she'd said, frosting the cake.

"Sam, can we assume that you're accepting our offer?" she'd asked on their phone call that morning, just before he was leaving to meet Jane Chapnick at Family Court. "We need an answer today."

Sam had come to the conclusion that he could have it both ways. Like many other law school students who discover the world of money as corporate law firm summer associates, it occurred to him that he could work at Fishbein for a couple of years, quickly pay down his debt and build some savings, before transferring to the public interest work that would feed his soul.

"I'm in," was all he had to say. Matriarch Connie's well-funded magic had worked once again.

And Jane Chapnick grudgingly accepted the decision. Not that she had much choice. As she hailed a taxi for the trip back to campus, she did have one parting thought for Sam.

"Mothers Need Lawyers could compete for your heart, but not your wallet," she said. She would wait for an opportunity to reargue this matter another day. Public interest lawyers like Jane Chapnick are in it for the long haul. For now, she would start thinking of Sam as a potential financial donor to her cause.

"Stay in touch, Sam," she said while sliding into the cab's back seat.

"You know I will," he replied, closing the door behind her. The cab shot into traffic, joining the thousands of other yellow taxis heading north on the five-lane avenue.

After a win in Family Court, accepting a big-money New York City corporate law future, and disappointing his favorite professor, Sam decided it was time for a few beers. He was a Wisconsin boy, after all, where big occasions are often marked by downing a cold one. Or two. Or many more.

Sam walked to the corner deli, and grabbed a six-pack of the most expensive beer in the cooler. He could now afford to pinch fewer pennies.

While waiting in line to pay, Sam noticed a stack of newspapers. The headline of *The New York Daily News*, in type far too large to be ignored, said "Corner Office a Deathtrap?" with the subhead, "Fishbein Founding Partner Albert Rose Dies in His Chair."

Two

Sam was on the phone with his Mom, again.

He was waiting for a telephoned zinger about his decision to join Fishbein, Schindler, Rose and Sampson. Some implied note of disapproval for forgoing public interest work. Some wisecrack about staying in New York City with all the rats on the treadmill. Something about selling out. But Barbara Mitcham wasn't playing along this time.

"I think you should do whatever makes you happy," she said. No judgment, no granted or denied approval, but one very practical question: "What are you going to do about clothes?"

"What do you mean?" he asked, knowing that for the past three years, like most law students, Sam Mitcham was not exactly a fashion plate. Ivy League or not, Columbia Law School meant t-shirts, jeans and sneakers, plus sweaters when it got cold. His "Clark Kent Corporate Look" wardrobe included two suits, five dress shirts, and six ties stored over a hanger somewhere in the back of Sam's closet. Such clothes were the uniform for interviews, and he made them do over his Fishbein associate summer. Why invest in a wardrobe until you have to?

"Real job, Sam," Barbara Mitcham said. "Time for an upgrade. Your sister can talk you through it, again."

"I hate shopping," he said. He was already missing the life of a law student.

"Just like your father," she replied.

"He had the right idea," Sam said. "If you need something, why not just find out where it's being sold, and go buy it? Not to mention filling up closets with clothes you don't wear."

"Your father never got 'shopping as recreation,' that's for sure," his Mom said. "But he did figure out that it's how a lot of attractive women spend their spare time."

"Duly noted," Sam said with a chuckle.

"Your sister is right here," Barbara Mitcham said, handing off the phone.

"Hey, Sam," Theresa said. "Do we get to spend your first Big Fish paycheck before you've even earned it?"

"Well, maybe a few things," Sam said. "I'm sure I'll need to wear suits every day now. How are you feeling?"

"I'm fine," she said. "Let's talk clothes." In this department, Theresa was every bit a match for Susan from Saks, though her client could not have provided a greater contrast to the Matriarchs.

A year ago, when it was evident he would need some business clothes for law firm interviews and a probable summer associate slot, Sam asked his sister for help. She recommended a shopping outing on Thanksgiving weekend, when they'd be together at home in Wisconsin anyway, and could take advantage of the "Black Friday" sales.

"Remember Black Friday?" Theresa said with a laugh.

"Never again," Sam replied, knowing he wasn't just talking about the early start time.

Many stores open early – REALLY early – on Black Friday. Retailers knew a strong showing the Friday after Thanksgiving was important for holiday sales, so they started opening their doors earlier and earlier. Four a.m. was not uncommon.

"Door buster prizes for the first 100 brave souls to rush the doors," Theresa said, also displaying selective memory about the event.

"And rush the doors they did," Sam said. "On New York's Long Island, someone actually got trampled to death. In Wisconsin, they were far more civil. A few heart attacks, tops."

With one hand pressing his cell phone to his ear, Sam looked at his meager closet. He vividly remembered that Black Friday when his sister scored two suits, five shirts, six ties, two belts, and three pairs of shoes. "At least 70 percent less than you'd pay in New York," she'd said proudly. He had to admit, even with his limited knowledge of shopping and retail price points, she was right. Cash on the table he understood, even if he did not understand the recreational appeal of shopping.

But that Black Friday a year ago was black for another reason. His sister Theresa had noticed a lump in her breast a few weeks before, and her doctor recommended a mammogram. "Nothing to worry about," she was told. "Eighty-five percent of women come back negative for cancer." Theresa lost the lottery that year. On Black Friday, she landed in the 15 percent positive group.

A lumpectomy, chemotherapy, and radiation were just the start. Then came more chemotherapy, and more radiation. It wasn't easy to watch someone he loved enduring the horrors of aggressive breast cancer, not to mention its prescribed treatment.

To the uneducated, the process of treating cancer with poison, namely arsenic oxide, looked crude at best. But in the past year Theresa, Barbara and Sam Mitcham became very educated very quickly. The treatment was often debilitating, but seemed the best that could be done in the situation.

Over the course of the year, for about as long as Sam wore his Black Friday wardrobe, the chemo and radiation continued. Most recently, it was declared a tentative success. Theresa was regaining her strength, there was no sign of recurring cancer, and her curly black hair was growing back. She was tired sometimes, but that seemed to be the only lingering symptom.

"OK, you've got a blue pin-stripe, and a charcoal suit," Theresa said on the phone, of course knowing his work wardrobe better than Sam did. "I think a solid blue and a solid black will be the next steps, probably tropical wool," she said. "Give me a call when you get to Barney's Warehouse."

"Dreading this, love you both," Sam said, about to hang up.

"Have a beer first," Theresa said, knowing her little brother would.

Sam treated himself to a couple of beers with lunch, rationalizing the intake as a way to build courage to shop. A quarterly clearance of the stock from Barney's, one of New York's trendiest stores, and Sam knew it would be a struggle just to get through the door. Thousands of suits, thousands of shirts, thousands of ties at a heavily-promoted Warehouse Sale in a giant former Chelsea factory space. What looked like the entire population of suburban New Jersey was inside, mostly corporate men being led around by wives and girlfriends.

With the benefit of the multiple beers, Sam wondered if any of these other GQ Magazine wannabees came from firms where a founding partner was just found dead. He certainly wasn't going to tell his Mom or sister about it until he knew what was going on. And for himself, for now, it would be easier to focus on the shopping than the even more unpleasant prospect that he made the wrong choice between Mothers Need Lawyers and the corporate behemoth of Fishbein, Schindler, Rose and Sampson.

Sam knew Theresa's instructions by heart, and dutifully went to the 42R racks, all 20 of them. The expert salespersons could smell reluctant neophyte shoppers like Sam, and he was grateful when a saleswoman touched his arm and said, "What do you need, honey?" After a quick explanation, he pressed speed dial number two, handed off his cell phone to the saleswoman, and trusted the shopping authorities to work it out.

"Turns out you're a 42-Regular for the American suits, but more a 40 for the way the Italian suits are cut this year," Theresa cheerily said when the saleswoman passed the cell phone back to Sam.

"Why do I need to know that?" Sam asked.

Forty minutes later, he was waiting in line to buy a solid blue, a solid black, and a bonus medium blue number that the saleswoman and Theresa agreed was too good a buy to pass up.

The shopping expedition, managed as it was, was exhausting to Sam. He had little energy for anything else that day, except another beer and a cursory look at the national law students' blog, "Raising the Bar."

One posted update caught Sam's eye. The story had quickly disappeared from the pages of *The New York Daily News*, replaced by more recent tales of intrigue, wrongdoing and scandal. But goings-on at the firm of Fishbein, Schindler, Rose and Sampson were always of interest to the readers and bloggers of Raising the Bar, since the audience wanted to work there, or at least be close to the firm's power and money:

"Death of Albert Rose Still Under Investigation," it said, but then suggestively asked, "Did the Man Who Invented the 'Poison Pill' Swallow One Himself?"

The blog post noted that along with Rose, two of the other founding partners – Fishbein and Schindler – died "on the job" within the past 10 years. The remaining partner, Oscar Sampson, was unavailable for comment.

J.D. FOX

Three

Sam always remembered first days, all the way back to his first day of grade school.

And, what he remembered most was the food. At his Wisconsin grade school, the first day menu always included Sloppy Joes, a combination of hamburger, tomato sauce and spices on a bun that the kitchen could knock out quickly in the frantic mess of a school's first day. To a six-year-old, it was predictable, great-tasting comfort food.

Almost 20 years had passed since those first-day Sloppy Joe lunches, and Sam wondered what awaited him, and what he'd get to eat, on his first day as a new associate at Fishbein, Schindler, Rose and Sampson.

But before the first lunch, he'd have to get through the first Monday morning.

"You got an ID?" said the guard, who looked to Sam as though he'd been behind the desk for years. Sam didn't recognize him from his summer as a Big Fish associate.

"I'm brand new," Sam said.

"Then I'll take your driver's license," said the guard.

Sam's name, and the name of every other starting associate, was on a list at the security desk on the ground floor. No one gets into a Manhattan office building without going through at least one security check, a legacy of 9-11.

In the mammoth office building in New York City's Times Square, the offices of Fishbein, Schindler, Rose and Sampson were on top. The top 35 floors of a 70-floor building. The publisher of the women's fashion magazine "Runway" occupied the lower half.

Though he had been to the office at least 60 times before as a summer associate, he got there a little early on his first "real" associate day to see if there had been any changes.

Nothing had changed, except the individual guard on duty that morning. The security desk for Fishbein was on the left of the massive lobby, in front of Fishbein-designated top-half elevators. The security desk and elevators for Runway were on the right. The power suits went to the left, the emaciated fashionistas went to the right.

Sam had a friend who did freelance graphic design at Runway, and last summer she took him to the cafeteria there. It didn't have the views of Fishbein's top floor eatery, but it did boast design by one of the nation's top architects. Sam had to laugh as he remembered the Runway cafeteria – beautiful design, ample and stylish food, but no one really ate.

Fashion models and the industry that starves them, he thought. The best part was the bank of undulating mirrors at the exit of the Runway cafeteria: just like the mirrors at a circus carnival, but designed so that no one looked any wider, just thinner. Always thinner.

Sam's gaze shifted from the lobby's Runway side to the Fishbein side, from the beautiful to the powerful.

"Okay, kid, you're good to go," said the guard. "Have a nice career."

Sam laughed, breezed through the metal detector, and made his way to Human Resources on the 36th floor.

Day One for anyone at Fishbein meant sitting through a sexual harassment video, listening to an overview on company policies and procedures, signing up for insurance benefits, and initialing lots of confidentiality agreements.

"Just one more," the Human Resources intern kept saying, "Then we'll get IDs and go to lunch." Orientation for new associates was an intern function. No need to waste the salaried help on this.

With 900 attorneys in New York, and another 600 at offices around the world, the Human Resources department at Fishbein had a lot of people to keep track of. And, especially at the staff level, there was plenty of turnover. Two people devoted 100% of their time to taking photos and making identification cards for the other 1,498 employees.

A laminated photo ID card included a magnetic stripe with the employees' encoded personnel information. It could be instantly read by the key-swipe locks guarding every wing on every floor. Sam figured he'd have to swipe his ID card at least three times to get from the lobby to wherever his desk was going to be. Security was tight at The Big Fish.

Sam didn't know yet that every time a card was swiped, a notation was made on the security computer system, recording the employee, the location, the date, and the time. Management could always check on employee comings and goings.

What Sam did know was that his just-issued Fishbein ID photo looked even worse than the one on his New York State Driver's License, and that his stomach was starting to growl with hunger.

Lunchtime. Though most of the first-day associate crop had been in the building before as summer employees, the Human Resources intern dutifully led the whole group up to the 60th floor cafeteria.

"I've already checked on the day's lunch specials," chirped the young Human Resources intern. Sam felt a little guilty at not paying attention to the intern's nametag, but figured he'd never see her again.

"Your choices include salad with unlimited toppings, fresh

roasted turkey at the carving station, and baked cod."

Sam was half-hoping for a Sloppy Joe.

Like many New York City law firms, Fishbein offered a variety of subsidized amenities designed to keep attorneys and staff from ever wandering outside the building. It worked. Who wouldn't eat lunch inside the Fishbein cafeteria for half the cost of any sandwich shop outside, not to mention avoiding the crush of tourists?

And then there was the view. At 60 stories up, atop the highest office tower in Times Square, the Fishbein cafeteria had a commanding view of Lower Manhattan to the south, the Hudson River and New Jersey to the west, and Midtown to the east. Sam couldn't see his own apartment building, but he could see the Italian restaurant four doors away from his place.

More significant than the skyline, today's view included the Matriarchs, all at one table at one time. Laura, Mindy, Carol and Connie.

Sam thought that unlike the young girl intern, these names would be worth memorizing: *Laura, Mindy, Carol and Connie*. It would be hard to distinguish them, though, since they all wore similar clothes. Navy, grey and black suits. Pastel shirts. Shoes that matched the suits. Sam thought they probably shopped together.

Perhaps, Sam thought, they're all meeting to share their grief over the recent death of Albert Rose. He'd seen another mention of the investigation on the legal blogs that morning. But the Matriarchs did not seem consumed by grief. Their mood seemed jubilant, almost celebratory.

"Go ahead, try it on," said Laura, to the new Matriarch.

Sarah, Fishbein's Director of Marketing and Business Development, was about to join the club. Since this was being done in the cafeteria, it was obviously intended for everyone to see, and spread the word.

"It's the most beautiful ring I've ever seen," Sarah said, clearly thrilled with her promotion. Sam didn't know anything about women's jewelry, but the stones on the fingers of the five women were certainly the largest diamonds he had ever seen. Sarah dabbed the tears from her eyes with a linen handkerchief. Her nose was running a little too.

"C'mon, pass it around," Mindy said playfully to Sarah. Each Matriarch, in turn, put the new ring up to her own for a mock inspection. From his vantage point several tables away, the stones appeared almost too large to be real. It looked like the gaudy costume jewelry Sam's sister Theresa wore when she was a little girl.

But Sam knew the rocks were real, and enormously expensive. As his sister and shopping expert would have said, "Probably mid-six figures."

Sam's Mom had an engagement ring and wedding band that were more metal than diamond, a reflection of his parents' modest pocketbooks at the time they became a couple.

Sam knew the women of Fishbein, Schindler, Rose and Sampson wore diamonds reflecting their level of accomplishment and influence within the world of corporate law. It was how they visibly kept score, he had heard. Junior female partners wore modest diamond rings. Senior female partners wore larger diamonds. But only the Matriarchs wore the trademark enormous, square-cut, rare, pale blue rocks. Sam wondered if the rings were heavy, but guessed the Matriarchs would gladly carry any burden to convey their hard-earned membership in this very exclusive club. Sarah must've done something recently to merit her inclusion.

"So, have you heard how they got started?" asked the HR intern, lightly working her fork around a salad at the table with Sam and the other new associates.

"Is this part of our orientation?" Sam asked in a whisper, realizing they were technically within earshot of the Matriarchs table.

"It's certainly not a secret," the intern said. "We usually get asked about it, and our director says it's fine to talk about the firm's history and culture. It's what makes us special."

"Who's your director?"

"Carol," said the intern, nodding in the direction of one of the Matriarchs sitting five feet away.

"Matriarch Carol?" asked one of the other new hires, while Sam reminded himself of the roster: *Laura, Mindy, Carol, Connie … and now Sarah.*

"She's a great boss," the intern said. "I'm learning so much from her."

"We're all ears," Sam said, speaking for the rest of the table, wondering if the intern knew Matriarchs lore he hadn't heard himself last summer.

"Laura has been here the longest," said the still-nameless intern. "She was the protégé of Mr. Fishbein, the first founding partner." Sam had heard that part.

"A sisterhood of women leading the firm was Laura's idea, but Mr. Fishbein encouraged her every step of the way. A man ahead of his time." Sam had heard that part, too.

"Mr. Fishbein actually acquired those amazing rings as payment from a delinquent client," added the intern. Sam hadn't heard that part.

"Certainly makes The Big Fish unique," Sam said with a smile.

The intern frowned. "We don't encourage that moniker," she said. By her use of the word "moniker," Sam knew the line was rehearsed. The message was clear – no joking about the Big Fish. At least not around the Matriarchs.

"What is the firm saying about the death of Albert Rose?" Sam asked, gambling that the intern wouldn't remember his name any more than he would remember hers.

"Isn't that tragic?" said the intern, and added, "Since it just happened, we haven't heard any direction yet from Carol."

"Probably not much to say," said Sam, looking over at the happy Matriarchs, remembering the blog speculation that the man who had invented the Poison Pill had been fed one himself. *Wicked way to manage a partnership*, Sam thought.

Halfway through his cut-rate carved turkey sandwich, Sam thought to check his cell phone. He hadn't been issued a work phone yet, though he knew that was coming. He had silenced the ringer on his personal phone, and jammed it in his pocket before leaving the apartment that morning.

The light on his cell phone was flashing, indicating a single voice mail delivered mid-morning. He had probably been filling out an insurance form when it came in. Since the phone said the message had been from his Mom, and she wouldn't call on his first day without good reason, he removed himself from the Matriarch-watching to retrieve the message.

Barbara Mitcham's message included some words, but mostly sobs. Sam had to listen a couple of times to understand what she was saying through the crying:

"We just got back from the doctor's office," said his Mother's anguished recording. "Theresa has leukemia."

Four

"What the hell happened?" was all that came out of Sam's mouth when his Mom picked up the phone.

Barbara Mitcham's sobs were gone. They'd been replaced by the steely resolve of a mother who had two children to guide and comfort.

"We didn't think it was that big of a deal," she said. "Theresa's been feeling a little run down lately, but we're used to that."

"Jesus, I was just on the phone with her buying clothes," Sam said. "She was fine."

"Theresa is not fine, Sam. The biopsy says she has acute leukemia, and her white blood counts are through the roof. They're about to put her on intense chemo."

The news hit quickly. It took more than a little of his inherited calm-under-pressure for Sam to maintain the composure of a Fishbein first-day associate. "What can I do?" he said quietly. "Should I come home?"

Barbara Mitcham had anticipated her son's question, and was ready with the answer. "No, stay right where you are. There's nothing you can do here. What this family does *not* need is you unemployed. It's your first day. Go back to work, and we'll talk later."

Sam put away his cell phone, and went back to the table of new associates. Ten minutes after Sam was delivered by the chatty HR intern to his new cubicle, and told to check his new computer's password and Fishbein's e-mail system, he was online researching Acute Myeloid Leukemia (AML) – his sister's new diagnosis.

The various leukemia information websites were about as comforting as they could be for patients who'd just received terrible news. AML, they said, is a fast-growing cancer of the blood and bone marrow. The abnormal leukemic cells grow quickly and crowd out the healthy ones. Of course, it's serious, often deadly.

Sam was quickly searching the sixth leukemia link from his initial search, when a suit appeared beside his cubicle. Sam looked up to a familiar face; a guy he'd seen but hadn't met during his summer as a Fishbein associate.

"Hi, I'm Robert. I'll be your guide to the Wonderful World of Fishbein, Schindler, Rose and Sampson." Robert looked to be about five nine, with thinning hair and wire frame glasses, and was too skinny for the suit he was wearing. *He could've used someone like Theresa Mitcham to buy his clothes*, Sam thought. *Too bad she was busy getting chemo.*

Sam made an immediate calculation to suck it up, and return Robert's questionable charm. Robert was probably a third- or fourth-year associate, Sam figured, an ambitious guy a couple of years ahead of him. Anyone in that slot, Sam knew, would be making a terrific salary, but wasn't a bright enough star to be designated obvious partner material. Robert was probably stuck, for now, proving his worth by handling a significant caseload, and supervising a few of the newbies.

"I stand, or actually sit, ready and eager to serve." Not Sam's best possible line, but it was his first day, and he'd been obviously distracted. Sam tried to purse his lips into something resembling a smile.

"Since you spent a summer here, I'm guessing you already know a fair amount about our world-renowned Restructuring Practice, the flip side of the world's best Mergers and Acquisitions

Practice?" Robert said, with an insincere smile of his own.

"Yes, sir," Sam said, keeping up his end. His first day, news of a sick-again sister, and this guy wanted to play verbal badminton?

"The world's largest corporations come to Fishbein, Schindler, Rose and Sampson when they want to marry. Excuse me, I mean when they have a proposed merger or acquisition requiring expert counsel," Sam said, trying to keep the awkward ball in the air.

"And the flip side?" Robert said, prompting the bright-yet-sarcastic Ivy League law scholar to translate his inner knowledge of corporate law.

"And the world's largest corporations, when they need to break into smaller, more efficient units, a process sometimes known as 'bankruptcy' but with 'restructuring' as a more palatable synonym, come to Fishbein, Schindler, Rose and Sampson for expert counsel."

Sam flashed back to the times in law school seminars when he'd been caught napping by a professor incapable of holding anyone's interest. Sam could always think of something to say, and say it very quickly. He was a natural lawyer. It always worked. He always got away with it. Sam even managed a toothy smile for Robert, motivated by the memory.

"I think you demonstrate a solid grasp of the business," said a sort-of-beaming Robert. "One more question. Who gets paid first after a merger, or after a restructuring?"

"Well, that would be Fishbein, Schindler, Rose and Sampson, sir," Sam said. "For expert counsel, without which corporate marriages and divorces could not happen."

Sam's attempt to reciprocate the forced intimacy was flying high, with Robert clearly enjoying the banter. So, Sam threw in one more: "It's the rule of law, upon which our very profitable economic system is based."

Sam paused, *wait for it*, he thought, then added, "Of course, rule of law means rule by lawyers."

That one earned a belly laugh from Robert, who'd always

wanted something to rule.

Robert then shifted his attention from the general to the specific in a way that would test the chops of any new associate: he started ripping into the Matriarchs.

"Now, this venerable firm has four named partners. How many of those named partners were men?

"All four," Sam said.

"How many left this firm, not to mention this life, within the past 10 years?"

"Three," Sam said, already wary at Robert's turn of the conversation into dark territory.

"How many died recently?"

"One."

"How many of them are still alive?"

"One."

"How many of the firm's executive officers, who actually run the business, are men?"

"I think none," Sam said.

"That is correct," Robert said. "You've heard of the Matriarchs?"

"Of course. Everyone has heard of them. Laura, Mindy, Carol, Connie and Sarah. They built the firm. Under the leadership of Messrs. Fishbein, Schindler, Rose, and Sampson, of course."

Robert was impressed that the new associate on his first day had noticed the promotion of his friend Sarah to the Matriarchs.

"Yes, they did. With a significant body count, namely those founding partners whose names are still on the front door, plus many others," Robert said. "Let me give you a lesson on your first day that most of them didn't learn until it was too late. Watch your back around the Matriarchs."

Sam found himself baffled for the second time in one day. Hot on the heels of Theresa's leukemia diagnosis, this completely unsubtle warning. He looked up at Robert, who was no longer smiling. *Why say all this to a lowly associate, on his first day?* Sam thought.

The awkward silence was broken by Robert's secretary, who ran up to the cubicle.

"Laura's on the phone, Robert. I told her you'd call her back, but she said I should find you. She's waiting."

"What have you heard about Laura?" Robert asked Sam.

"I just heard at lunch that she started it all. Joined the firm 20-plus years ago, recruited the other Matriarchs as the firm grew. Just promoted Sarah to the group, so now there are five of them."

Robert hadn't waited for Sam's response, running away from the cubicle to his office. He shut the door behind him.

Sam kept an eye out for Robert, but the door stayed closed. Sam's attention returned to his Fishbein computer, switching back and forth between the firm's intranet employee procedure manuals, and the far more compelling leukemia information websites. His eye occasionally looked over to one of the other cubicles, occupied by another first-day associate. She hadn't said a word at lunch, but Sam remembered her nametag: *Sandi*.

She hadn't come from his law school. She was attractive. Sam's sister would've approved of her first-day wardrobe; the lady knew how to dress. Theresa would've told him that Sandi wore a lot of Ann Taylor outfits – perfect for the office, but still fashionably up-to-date. Today's selection included a skirt with a slit up the side.

Sandi smiled a little in Sam's direction, which Sam thought meant she probably heard the exchange with Robert. Or maybe she liked him. Or maybe she thought he was ballsy for asking questions about the Matriarchs at their orientation lunch. Maybe all three. Who knew? A lot had happened today. Sam smiled back, a little, one of those pressed smiles of shy men from the Midwest. Sandi glanced back to her computer. Initial exchange over.

Time passed. Robert stayed in his office. Sam kept flipping between the business of Fishbein and his own family. The Fishbein stuff was rote; the leukemia information was depressing.

At around 6 p.m., the office started to clear out. The first-day associates in their cubicles looked to the long-serving legal secretaries for guidance as to the acceptable exit time.

"I think we're clear for the day," Sandi said. "And it looks as though they're taking a special early interest in you."

"You heard it all?" Sam asked.

"Yeah, Robert apparently likes to disclose a lot of information up front," she said. "He was gauging your reaction. Not too subtle."

"Your test will probably come tomorrow," Sam said. "Robert can only handle one newbie initiation per day."

"That'll help me sleep tonight," she said. Her smile grew a little.

"Going to the subway?" he asked. Sam wasn't sure what was registering on his face, but his Dad taught him to always default to the *charm* setting.

Sandi responded in kind. "Yeah, let's go," she said. "We can help each other find the exit from this place."

With their first official day completed, Sam walked Sandi the one block to the Times Square subway station at 42nd Street and 7th Avenue, dodging tourists each step of the way. They hesitated at the top of the stairs, and then parted with the nod of new colleagues.

"Shall we do all this again tomorrow?" she asked.

"I think we've signed on for longer than that," he said.

"Yeah, I think we have," Sandi replied.

She went down the stairs to the trains, disappearing into the commuter crowd. Sam stayed on the sidewalk for the short walk west to his Hell's Kitchen apartment. Once he got inside the door, Sam threw his jacket on the couch and went back online. He had already planned his next few moves. On a new Fishbein associate's salary, he could easily afford the cheap weekend airfare to go home.

Five

"You shouldn't have come, there's nothing you can do."

Sam expected to hear that from his mother as soon as he joined her in the hospital's waiting room. He'd left his Hell's Kitchen apartment Saturday morning at 5:00, got to LaGuardia by 5:30, and made the short flight to Milwaukee without a hitch.

Sam had done enough research to know that his sister Theresa had now effectively lost the lottery twice – her type of breast cancer occurred in just 15% of women who develop a lump. Of that group, a much smaller number develop leukemia "secondary" to their breast cancer.

"How's she feeling?" Sam asked his Mom.

"She's weak, she's tired, she's depressed. Who can blame her?"

"When can I see her?" he asked. They were alone in the waiting room of the hospital. It was, after all, Saturday morning. Barbara Mitcham filled her son in on what details she knew. They'd both become relative experts in the treatment of breast cancer, but leukemia on top of that was a shock.

"Leukemia secondary to breast cancer," Sam said, first to his mother and then to the oncologist who joined them for an update. "Does that mean she developed leukemia because of all the chemo and radiation she had?"

"Probably," said the oncologist. "The treatment for breast cancer is very strong. Because her breast cancer was so aggressive, our treatment had to be aggressive as well." The oncologist had the calm yet intelligent manner of a doctor who delivered a lot of bad news, but who always tried to combine the reality with hope. "When we go after breast cancer, we're taking down the patient's immune system, and a lot of healthy cells, at the same time. Fortunately, most women respond well to the treatment."

If you count losing your hair and feeling like hell for months, Sam thought, but he knew that everyone in this conversation was on the same side. The available treatment was the available treatment.

"What's next?" Sam wondered aloud.

"More chemo and radiation, for now," the oncologist said.

"And prayer," Barbara Mitcham said.

The oncologist said she'd allow Sam to see Theresa, since he was an immediate family member. But, she said with an almost clinical aloofness, "you'll have to observe precautions. We're taking her immune system down to zero."

Proper precautions around a new leukemia patient meant not only hand washing, which Sam had been instructed to do as soon as he entered the ward, but putting on a surgical gown, gloves and mask. It felt to Sam like he was putting on an astronaut's moon suit.

"One more thing," the oncologist said. "I'm sorry, but you can't touch her. Too much risk of infection."

The reality of the current situation didn't really hit Sam until he and his Mom donned paper gowns, latex gloves, and itchy masks. He could see a few tears already welling up in his Mom's eyes as they prepared to enter Theresa's room. Sam was determined to be the strong man for his family. He certainly didn't feel that way, but was confident he could put the lawyer's mask of confident authority over his more genuine reactions of sadness and fear.

Theresa looked like an old man. Her hair had already been shaved; they'd learned from previous experience that it was better to take it off than watch it fall out. Her face was devoid of color. Her cheeks were sunken. She was hooked up to a few IVs, and because of the infection risk the room lacked any humanizing adornment – no flowers, certainly no cheer.

"Hey," she drowsily said, not really surprised to see her baby brother after the latest news. "How's the well-dressed legal eagle?"

"I'm wearing one of your suits underneath this gown," Sam said, having already decided to keep this visit as light as he could. "The jacket's a little tight for a Saturday, but one must maintain the proper tone at Fishbein, Schindler, Rose and Sampson."

"Tight-assed lawyers," she said, and Sam could almost hear their Mom's eyebrows rising under her mask. Before any other conversation about Sam's new job, Theresa exercised the hospital patient's prerogative to address the illness.

"Doesn't this suck?" she said, summarizing everything about her life over the past year.

"This totally sucks," Sam acknowledged. "How do you feel?"

"I'm so tired. Nothing hurts, but I'm so tired." She looked like she was about to cry. Sam started to bite his lip, but she quickly brightened. "And then there's the throwing up all the time, which is doing wonders for my dating prospects."

Sam's smile showed even with his face obscured by a surgical mask, but his mind couldn't help running through the checklist of horrors his sister had endured over the past year. The startling lump. The Black Friday diagnosis. The lumpectomy. The chemo. The radiation. The hair loss. The nausea. The vomiting. It just went on and on, and now they were faced with so much more.

"But hey, I'm still here," Theresa said.

"Still here, and not going anywhere," her little brother said. *So far so good*, he thought. Everyone was keeping it together. And no one was mentioning how much this hospital room looked like

Larry Mitcham's hospice room, in those agonizing weeks before Sam and Theresa's father passed away.

They'd only been talking a few minutes, but Theresa was obviously tired, so Sam and Barbara Mitcham retreated to the waiting room to begin the weekend vigil. Whenever she wanted them, they'd be a few steps away.

It didn't really surprise Sam when the signal light on his portable phone/e-mail unit started to flash. As he explained to his mother, the phone belonged to the firm. It even had a special slang name, the Fish Fone. All the new associates had been issued one in their first week, so they could always be available, no matter where they were. In Sam's case, it was so that he could be available to his edgy supervisor, Robert.

Sam knew he was taking a calculated risk leaving New York after just his first week at The Big Fish, and not telling anyone. Not that there was a choice. How could he not be with his family? His mother had told him not to come, but both she and Theresa were clearly relieved that he made the effort. As for work, if something came up, there was the Fish Fone. Or he could go to an internet café if there was a long document to review. Worst case, he'd head back early.

The e-mailed message on his Fish Fone was indeed from Robert. Luckily, no voice mail, which would have indicated a higher alert. This first one was a minor technical question about one of the drudge-work documents he had thrown at Sam a few days ago. Sam suddenly felt like he was back in law school, fielding a question by a professor just checking to see if he was staying awake.

Barbara Mitcham wasn't impressed by the Fish Fone, or with a new job which included first-weekend fire drills. "This isn't that big of a deal," Sam told her. "Robert is probably sending e-mails to all his new charges, and keeping score as to who writes back and when."

"So why don't you just send him the answer and get it over with?" she said.

"Because I don't want to have an all-weekend electronic conversation with a guy who does this instead of having a life," Sam said. It was a rushed conclusion, based on what Sam actually knew about Robert's life…but probably accurate. Robert was in that grey zone, not a new associate but not a partner-track star either. He spent his days trying to impress people like the Matriarchs and the firm's partners, yet shifting as much of the real work as he could to the newbies. And celebrating the promotion of his friend Sarah to the Matriarchs.

Sam waited an hour, then sent Robert a reply not only explaining the question, but the next steps that might be appropriate to serve their restructuring client.

Robert's reply was almost instant: "Thx," it read.

"What does that mean?" Barbara Mitcham asked.

"It's e-mail shorthand, acknowledging my response, not questioning it yet not necessarily agreeing with it. I think it's mostly a message that I'm always on call, especially on weekends, for the clients of Fishbein, Schindler, Rose and Sampson," Sam said.

"He sounds like a piece of work," said Sam's often-blunt Mom.

"Yeah, I think I'm working with a bunch of them. Both the men and the women."

"Quite a contrast with the Columbia Child Advocacy Clinic, and Mothers Need Lawyers," his Mom said.

"Thanks for the reminder," Sam replied.

The short hospital weekend settled into a quick routine. Gowns and masks on, spend a little time with Theresa until she started to flag, then back to the waiting room. Down to the cafeteria for food and coffee. Back to see Theresa in the moon suits. After a few rounds, home for some sleep, then back again on Sunday morning.

There were a few more annoying e-mailed questions from Robert, but nothing that threatened Sam's ability to spend the weekend at the hospital.

The stoic composure they maintained as a family held through this initial round of leukemia diagnosis and its aggressive treatment. It was only in the weekend's last meeting, as Sam was about to depart for the airport, that his sister summed up her reaction to what had happened.

"Sam," she said, "Don't count on anything."

Six

The security system at Fishbein was far more intense than anything Sam encountered in airports over the weekend. He offered to take off his shoes at Fishbein's front desk, but the security guard didn't appreciate the joke first thing Monday morning. Sam swiped in once in front, once outside the elevator on his floor, and a third time outside his corridor before making it to his cubicle by 8:30 a.m.

Sam hadn't had much sleep. The plane from Wisconsin to LaGuardia took off a few hours late Sunday night, but he finally boarded for the short flight east. He figured he'd pulled it off. The magic of the Fish Fone ensured he was nearly as accessible 1,500 miles away in the Midwest as he would be down the hall.

A clean weekend break, with one exception.

"You look as though you haven't slept much since I saw you last," Sandi said from the next cube. Sam mumbled something about staying up late to watch old movies with the guys, but she knew something was up. He didn't know her well enough to tell her anything else. And his Midwestern reticence certainly wouldn't permit any comment on Sandi's Monday outfit, and how it complimented her figure, though he'd be keeping an eye on that all day.

Sam knew that Sandi was as smart as he was, but not quite as lucky. She didn't get into the Ivy League as he had. Sandi was a graduate of Fordham Law School, also in New York City – a well-regarded law school, but it wasn't Columbia. She'd made the best of it. They both had multiple jobs offers, which is better than some of their classmates did in a volatile job market.

Fishbein's recruiting strategy pursued both the bulk of Columbia's first tier, and the cream of Fordham's second. Matriarch Connie, the recruiting director, often noted that she'd rather recruit a second-tier student like Sandi than a first-tier student like Sam. Sandi was hungrier. Just as intelligent. Just less fortunate during the law school application derby, which was four years ago and would soon be ancient history.

"Good morning, Legal Eagles," said Robert. He was followed by two secretaries, each holding a bundle of files. One pile went to Sam, the other to Sandi. "Here's some of the lower-level legal review attached to the DeSantis restructuring," he said. "I know it will test your considerable skill to review these crucial documents, and log them into the case docket."

Sandi summed up their second-week assignment as soon as Robert and his minions sauntered away. "Mindless base-covering for which our troubled client will pay about a thousand dollars an hour," she said.

Sam smiled, knowing he might be seated next to not only a beautiful workmate, but one who shared his level of respect for the drudgery that comprises the majority of corporate legal work.

Hours passed, the piles of files were reviewed and logged, and Robert returned. "We need to go see Laura," he said.

"We, as in you and me?" asked Sam. Sandi shared his disbelief. Matriarch Laura wanted to see Sam?

"Let's go, Sam," said Robert. "When Laura says jump, we ask 'how high?'"

"Maybe it's something good," Sandi said, trying to sound optimistic.

Both Sam and Robert glared at her. "Perhaps this is an opportunity to expand your knowledge base," said Robert. "How much do you know about Laura Henderson?"

"She joined Fishbein, Schindler, Rose and Sampson right out of a paralegal program in the '80s," Sandi said. "The firm had by then already made its name as one of the world's premier corporate law firms, and her timing couldn't have been better – the wave of mergers and acquisitions in the '70s and '80s meant there was plenty of work for everyone." She smiled politely.

Sam and Robert's mouths dropped simultaneously. Sandi was at least as smart as they were.

"Do continue," Robert said.

"Firms like Fishbein pioneered many of the era's edgiest tactics," she said, "including the offensive 'hostile takeover' and defensive 'poison pill.' Laura was an ambitious, aggressive and smart woman in the right place at the right time."

"We understand that the recently-deceased Albert Rose personally invented the poison pill," Sam added. "Which made him a legend among corporate lawyers."

"Laura's not a lawyer." Robert said. "She never concentrated on cases at all."

"What did she do?" Sam asked.

"At first, her power was derivative. She worked long hours, and never said no to anything. Nights, weekends, travel, whatever … Laura was there, was competent, and always asked for more," said Robert. "After he tested her a few times with progressively more difficult personnel projects, she became the indispensable right hand to Morris Fishbein, the first founding partner."

"I did hear a few stories about him," Sam said. "Morris Fishbein had a nickname. No one at the firm back in the '70s was gutsy enough to say it to his face, but everyone knew it. They called him 'Napoleon.'"

"Judging by the portraits on the walls, he physically fit the bill," Sandi said.

"Yes, I've seen those pictures," said Robert, reminding Sam and Sandi that he had only been there a few years longer than they had. "Morris Fishbein was about five-foot-five. The son of New York City garment workers, immigrants from Eastern Europe. His parents poured everything they had into their only son, so he was raised with all the hope, expectation, and emotional baggage of a second-generation American immigrant. He was a natural and aggressive corporate lawyer."

"But he couldn't do it without Laura?" Sam asked.

"If Morris Fishbein had one problem, it was that the size of his brain was matched by the softness of his heart. He couldn't bring himself to discipline lawyers, let alone fire anyone," Robert said. "Yet he knew that to build a firm and a global business, he would need someone with an aptitude for the unpleasant tasks of management. That's where Laura came in."

"So with Morris Fishbein at the helm, and Laura Henderson at the broom to clean up the messes, they rode the wave of corporate megamergers," Sam said. "The firm was of counsel to one side or the other in most of the era's significant deals. Banks became global financial services conglomerates. Farm implement dealers morphed into agribusiness. Regional airlines became transportation networks. Morris Fishbein and Laura Henderson were a huge success, ending up with 900 lawyers, in 30 practice areas, in every major business center on the globe – except Africa."

"There's more. Have you heard this?" Robert asked. "Some firms went so far as to hire Fishbein to stay *out* of their deals, fearing the growing reputation of The Big Fish and its talent at helping one company swallow another."

Back in their respective law schools, Sam and Sandi read articles about a widely-practiced tactic from the era called "Sterilizing Morris." Other firms were so afraid of Morris that they paid The Big Fish to keep him away from their deals. Morris Fishbein just smiled; Laura cashed the checks.

"As smart and cunning as Morris Fishbein was during his prime, Laura Henderson managed to stay at his side, if not one step ahead," Sandi said. "And, over the next 20 years, she hired good executive help – three other women who headed legal recruiting, finance, case management, and now Sarah in marketing. The Matriarchs."

"But as the Matriarchs began to ascend, the founding partners had a different trajectory," Sam said. "Morris Fishbein passed away in 2000 at the age of 82. He worked right up to the end. His partners worked and went out the same way, albeit at much younger ages than Fishbein. David Schindler died in 2003, at the age of 66. Albert Rose, master of the poison pill, died at age 64."

"The Big Fish doesn't have a mandatory retirement age," Robert quipped.

"It doesn't seem to need one," Sam said.

"Right, but enough of that for now," Robert said. "Let's go see Laura."

"Good luck," Sandi said, as Robert and Sam tightened their ties.

No one used the stairways between floors at Fishbein. They went to the bank of elevators, and rode two flights up to the C-Suite. Sam didn't have to swipe his ID card on that floor, and doubted it would have admitted him anyway. Robert did the swiping, and held the heavy glass door to admit Sam.

Like most corporate law firms, Fishbein had an impressive array of modern art on its walls, mostly purchased at cut rates from struggling artists back in '70s and '80s. Impressive as the firmwide collection was, Sam noticed the really good stuff – including a few Picassos – was on the top floor. Fishbein's art was probably worth millions.

After the hallway art, Sam was a little underwhelmed at the sight of Laura's office. It was in the corner, of course, with amazing views of Lower Manhattan and even the Statue of Liberty. But the furnishings, although tasteful, weren't at all ostentatious. Perhaps Laura's cost-cutting acumen honed during a few layoffs got internalized. Or maybe she was so secure in her power that she didn't need to display it.

Laura was sitting behind her desk, occupied with her computer. Sam noticed her conservative yet trendy suit, and tried to remember his sister's fashion lessons. Armani? Maybe Chanel? She didn't look up when Sam and Robert entered, and just kept typing. *Probably answering e-mail from one of the other Matriarchs,* Sam thought.

The real surprise was the well-dressed man sitting on the couch. Sam had never met him, but recognized him from the firm's brochures. Impeccably tailored, probably a hand-made Italian suit. White collar. Subtle tie. Grey hair. It was Oscar Sampson, the one remaining founding partner. There was no opportunity to shake his hand, and he wouldn't look Sam in the eye. Oscar Sampson just sat on Laura's designer sofa, hands folded and eyes down.

Laura finished typing, and swiveled to address the three men in the room. She was evidently a woman of few words, especially since there was no one here she needed to impress.

"Robert, I appreciate your support of this idea, especially since Sam is so new," she said. "Sam, welcome to Fishbein, Schindler, Rose and Sampson."

He bowed, a little. Sam didn't know what to say, or if he should say anything at all.

With what amounted to her welcome out of the way, Laura reset Sam's priorities at the firm.

"I need just a little of your time to help on a special project with Oscar," she said. "It could involve some travel."

"I'd be happy to help," Sam said, not having the first clue what that would mean.

Seven

It's a lot nicer to fly from New York to the Midwest in first class than in coach.

Oscar Sampson hadn't flown coach in years. His choices were first class or private corporate jet. Going to Chicago in the small first class section was a step down from his normal routine. But then, these were difficult times.

The instructions from Laura had been brief, and Robert didn't have much to add.

"Oscar is a little rattled right now, what with the death of Rose and all," he'd said. "Go with him to Chicago, and do whatever he wants."

"And keep you posted?" Sam asked.

"That's what the Fish Fone is for," he said. "Oscar doesn't carry one. He doesn't want to, which is fortunate, because Laura doesn't want him to have one."

"Why me?" It was an obvious question, and Sam thought he could at least throw it out there, since Robert had previously been so blunt with him.

"Oscar and Peter DeSantis are old drinking buddies, and DeSantis Industries is about to go bankrupt. They'll need an audience for their war stories."

"I don't get it. I'm there to handle Oscar Sampson?"

"Your time will be fully billable to the DeSantis restructuring. Oscar needs someone to hold his hand. A pretty woman like Sandi would be too obvious. And, once Laura explained his options, Oscar actually picked you."

"I still don't get it."

"You don't have to. Pack a couple of suits, and get Oscar on the plane."

Sam didn't have anything to worry about on departure. Sampson had been a corporate lawyer for 40 years, and didn't miss planes. Planes had sometimes been held for him, but that was different. Sam hoped the older lawyer would provide some explanation of their agenda, or maybe give some hint about what he was dealing with since the death of his partner, Albert Rose. But once the morning flight boarded Oscar Sampson promptly fell asleep without saying a word.

"It's a short trip," said the flight attendant. With only 10 seats in first class, and most of them filled with already-dozing middle-aged executives, she could dote on the young lawyer. "Can I get you some breakfast?"

"Absolutely," Sam said. "What have you got?"

"I have omelettes, English muffins, hash browns, sausage, and bacon," she replied.

"Perfect," Sam said.

"Which ones?" she asked.

"All of them," Sam said, with a smile. "I'm just waking up."

First class travel was just one of the creature comforts Sam would come to know traveling with a founding partner of a major firm, especially one on a short leash. No flagging a cab once they got to Chicago's O'Hare International Airport, either. There was a chauffeur waiting for them.

The hotel, situated off Michigan Avenue in Chicago's Loop, was four-star. Maybe five. Sam never paid any attention to hotel star levels, because his previous out-of-town lodging was usually the extra bedroom at his Mom's house.

"We're meeting Peter DeSantis for lunch," Oscar said in the lobby. "Get a car for us at noon." Oscar Sampson was a distinguished-looking man. Sam wondered why he was being so blunt, but was in no position to question his authority.

"You bet, sir," seemed like the right thing for Sam to say.

"No need to call me sir, and no need to knock yourself out with the details," said the founding partner. "Just send Robert a message on that ridiculous Fish Fone contraption. Making the arrangements will be his top priority."

They parted at the elevator bank, but not before Oscar got in one shot betraying his 63-year-old world view: "I'm glad Morris Fishbein didn't live to see a telephone named after him."

"They do save time," said Sam.

"Good, you'll need it. Go throw your stuff in your room, send an urgent text to Robert, and I'll see you in 20 minutes."

Sam wasn't surprised when Robert responded instantly to his text message, confirming a car for the Sampson/Mitcham party at noon. The driver would be at their disposal for the day. Sam figured it would have been cheaper to just keep the airport chauffeur, but it was obvious that no one was limiting the expense account on this trip. After DeSantis Industries went into bankruptcy, its legal counsel at Fishbein, Schindler, Rose and Sampson would be paid first. Their meal and travel expenses, too.

"Sam, have you ever heard of the three-martini lunch?" was the first question Oscar Sampson asked when they got into the sumptuous new limo. Sampson was suddenly much nicer than on the plane.

"I think that was the norm in my Dad's era, but that was another day."

"Well, my boy, that day is back, at least for now." Sampson was smiling.

"This is your trip, your client, and your lunch. I'm here to help." Sam looked at his watch. One o'clock Eastern Time, high noon in Chicago. They weren't on their way to the company cafeteria.

"Peter DeSantis, it's my pleasure to present Sam Mitcham, the brightest star of our new associate class," Oscar said. The impeccably dressed, balding, moderately overweight Midwestern executive grabbed Sam's hand and shook it for a good five seconds.

"Sir, it's my pleasure," Sam said.

Oscar Sampson and Peter DeSantis had known each other for forty years, greeted each other warmly, and had top-shelf martinis served within five minutes of their arrival at the Chicago Mercantile Club. Even without the alcohol, they would've been two of the most charming businessmen Sam had ever met. With alcohol, they were positively memorable.

"You remember when it was just that crummy warehouse I inherited from my father?" Peter DeSantis said, beginning the trip through their mutual business memories.

"I remember it was a complete wreck, and we were faced with the choice of a shotgun wedding or a burial," Oscar replied.

Sam sipped his martini, trying to drink more slowly than his elders. And he remembered the DeSantis files. The first merger, 38 years ago, was with another struggling Chicago warehousing firm.

"I believe there were a series of small mergers before the combination with Addison Trucking," Sam said. "The Addison combination really put you on the map, along with its completely novel financing. And after that, at least one significant acquisition every two years."

Peter DeSantis looked at the young associate, and lifted his glass. "Oscar, your boys always come to the table prepared."

Sam passed the first test. He figured today's lunch was about the rosy past, not the rocky present. From the files, he also knew about the heavy debt load DeSantis assumed for its largest acquisition and the downhill stumble since then. Even Oscar Sampson wasn't a good enough lawyer to stop the fall. So here they were, talking about the glory days, but most pointedly not talking about the looming bankruptcy.

Another round of martinis appeared, then another. The Mercantile Club's ancient waiters would lovingly shake each martini with the perfect amount of ice, a time-honored ritual designed to amuse the Club's corporate lions. Three lawyers, three waiters, three martinis. *I could get used to this*, Sam thought.

Then the food started to arrive. Sam hadn't remembered ordering lunch. "They know what we like here," Oscar said. "I'm guessing the Wisconsin boy wouldn't mind a good steak."

"My Dad taught me that martinis and steak go together," Sam said, watching as three thick slabs were brought to the table. The Mercantile Club was known for its Grade AAA filet mignon, served medium rare unless a customer was foolish enough to request it prepared another way.

It was the best steak Sam had ever tasted. The prime cut of beef had to be at least 12 ounces, huge for a lunch portion. But a size that went well with three martinis. And sides of garlic mashed potatoes, creamed spinach, and homemade bread.

After eating more at lunch than he usually ate in a day, not to mention the drinks, Sam wondered if he'd have to find room for dessert. The Mercantile Club had a cart nearby loaded with luxurious sugar and cholesterol. Instead, the veteran waiters, who'd served DeSantis and Sampson after every major deal of the past four decades, brought a special decanter of cognac.

"Sam, you've read the files, but words can't begin to express my appreciation for all that Oscar Sampson has done for me," Peter DeSantis said, with what looked like real emotion on top of his martini and cognac buzz.

Sam took a sip of the fine brandy, and luckily had time to swallow before Oscar Sampson raised his own glass to toast:

"Thank you, Peter, and may I add that if I've reached the point in my own career where I require a handler for our meetings together, I could do worse than Larry and Barbara Mitcham's son."

Eight

"What the hell is going on?"

Sam almost shouted it into the phone at his Mom, realizing it was the second time he'd started a conversation this way. The last time, learning about Theresa's leukemia diagnosis, he'd been baffled. This time, he was angry.

"Why didn't you tell me you knew Oscar Sampson?"

"Tell you what?" his Mom asked. "Oscar and I went to high school together. He was a senior, I was a freshman. We've kept in touch. No big deal."

"You didn't think your history would be relevant to me taking a job at his firm?"

"Actually, I was kind of relieved. He always said that New York was full of sharks. I figured you could do worse than work for Oscar Sampson."

"Funny, he said *he* could do worse than to have Barbara Mitcham's kid as his handler."

"Why would Oscar Sampson need a handler? Isn't he the boss?"

"I gotta go," Sam said, as he hit the red "stop" button on his Fish Fone. He didn't technically hang up on his Mom, but it was close. After three martinis, nerves can fray quickly.

The red light on the Fish Fone started flashing, indicating an incoming call or text message. Sam knew it would be from Robert, with a post-lunch check-in. "How's M Club?" Robert texted. For all Sam knew, Robert could've been watching on a closed-circuit camera uplink.

"All's well. Client is happy." Sam kept the response brief, non-specific, and cheery. It was no more than a new associate could be expected to report from his first lunch with the old boys. The news would be immediately relayed to the old girls, the Matriarchs. Sam could only guess what else was on their agenda for Oscar and Peter DeSantis. Not to mention wondering about his own mother's role in all this.

Next stop, after the enhanced liquid lunch, was the corporate offices of DeSantis Industries. It took awhile for the limo to get them there, with client and counsel in the back seat sharing memories, and Sam in the front seat with the driver.

"By the way, kid, one more lesson from the Golden Era of Three Martini Lunches," Peter DeSantis said, patting Sam firmly on the shoulder from the back seat. "Always drink vodka. No one can smell it on your breath back at the office."

"Lesson learned, sir," Sam said, and since the driver laughed he did too.

The entourage was treated almost reverentially upon their arrival at the suburban office park. The security wasn't as tight as at Fishbein, but maybe that was the Midwest versus New York. The guards certainly knew Peter DeSantis, and a few also nodded at Oscar Sampson. The new kid was just the latest of Oscar's boys from New York, doing the legal grunt work.

Stumbling slightly as they entered the executive conference room, Sam was reminded that he'd just had three large martinis with lunch. He did a little math in his head. *What was that, maybe 12 ounces of pure alcohol?*

Whatever it was, it got Peter DeSantis and Oscar Sampson into even more of a talking mood once they settled into their leather chairs around the massive mahogany table. DeSantis motioned

Sam into one of many open chairs next to them.

"The business we built, DeSantis Industries, had actually started, and prospered, on an idea we wrote on the back of a napkin at another liquid lunch decades ago," the CEO said, laughing.

"Peter had a warehouse, a place to store manufactured products. It was losing money, and would've sunk if we hadn't taken drastic action," remembered his counsel.

"We thought, 'Why not build storage capacity, and then add transportation? The business could arrange pick-up, storage, and delivery, of almost anything. We could add refrigeration to handle perishable products.'"

They'd started with the lone warehouse Peter inherited, fortunately located on prime land in the Chicago suburbs; at the time it was becoming the major hub of American commerce.

The idea born over a few martinis paid off, immediately out of the gate. "Right place at the right time," as they would often toast each other. Toasting with vodka, to avoid any tell-tale odors back at the office. Building an empire should be fun, they agreed.

Peter DeSantis just kept talking. Sam was enjoying it, but wondered if DeSantis had started drinking before they met for lunch.

"First, there was a shotgun wedding with another struggling warehouse," DeSantis said. "I had a ledger sheet just marginally better than my target, and I bet my inheritance."

"Then, we started acquiring other warehouses, building a connected network first in the Midwest and then beyond," Oscar added. "At the same time, we leveraged the financing from each acquisition into the next acquisition."

Reflecting their huge appetite for compound risk along with steak and vodka, Sam thought.

Peter DeSantis scouted new prospects, and hired competent managers to run the day-to-day operations. Oscar Sampson, and his growing New York City corporate law firm, handled the financing, government filings, and blunted talk of antitrust action as the conglomerate grew.

Then came Addison Trucking -- built by another entrepreneur and another sharp corporate attorney. Perhaps some Chicago Mafia influence as well, but nothing that ever went to court.

"Do you want to hear about Addison?" Peter DeSantis asked.

"I'd love to. The history books are a little thin on that one," Sam replied.

"Addison Trucking was run, at least nominally, by Tony Addison. The time was right to sell, and he knew it," DeSantis said. "Tony Addison got a fat payout, which included a good share for himself once he'd taken care of his partners. We got a ready-made transportation arm, and didn't have to worry much about labor problems."

They could've called their new conglomerate anything, but it was over another three-martini lunch that Oscar said, "Why don't we call it DeSantis Industries? We're now just doing trucking and storage, but why not pick a name that allows for growth?" Peter DeSantis shared his lawyer's affinity for thinking big, and the new name was sealed over a toast: "Here's to DeSantis Industries," they said. "The sky's the limit."

Sam wondered why Oscar didn't attach his own name to the Chicago operation, but Oscar didn't have to. He was the brains behind the throne, and Peter DeSantis was a loyal business partner and real friend. Oscar could live in New York, coordinate the deals, and hop the DeSantis corporate jet to Chicago whenever needed. Just for lunch, sometimes.

"It worked so well for so long," DeSantis told Sam. Peter DeSantis became a rich and powerful man, even by Chicago standards. Oscar Sampson became one-fourth of a huge law firm, with three partners pulling at least as much weight, and bringing in as much business, as he did.

"As it turned out, Addison Trucking wasn't as great a combination as we'd hoped," Oscar said. "Tony Addison's operation looked amazing from the 30,000-foot level, and easily passed every due diligence test we could devise. But Tony Addison didn't take care of everyone in his exit package, and we lost a few friends in the process."

The cracks didn't show right away, in fact not for years. DeSantis Industries actually maintained robust growth, with at least one more acquisition every two years. Each bump in size meant another celebratory lunch at the Mercantile Club, and another reason for Fishbein, Schindler, Rose and Sampson to grow its Mergers and Acquisitions (M&A) practice.

Oscar had lost count, but Sam was probably the 20th new associate assigned to the DeSantis business over the years. But, as Sam knew, he was different on several counts. Oscar and Peter's old debts were coming due, and DeSantis Industries was heading for bankruptcy.

Peter DeSantis would likely lose his company, and a good chunk of his stock, in a restructuring. As was the case with most big bankruptcies, the name on the buildings would probably stay the same, to maintain "branding continuity," though the original owner would get the boot. Sam didn't know what Oscar's fate might be, but also knew the Matriarchs had assumed a significant role in the answer to that question.

"Sam, you've seen what I've built over 40 years. What do you think?" Oscar asked in the limo on the way back to the hotel.

"Well, the business is impressive, though currently troubled," Sam said. "As for me becoming your so-called handler, not to mention your history with my mother, you'll have to give me some time with that."

"Sam, you're a bright guy, come from good stock, and I got you into this for a reason. We don't have a lot of time, and you have to make a decision."

Oscar, knowing he had the full, now-sober attention of Barbara Mitcham's son, pushed his case: "I need a friend, a friend like I have in Peter DeSantis. Have you heard of the Matriarchs?"

"Of course I have," Sam said. "Everyone has."

"Well, the Matriarchs are bringing down my firm, and everything I've built," Oscar said. "People are getting hurt – literally – Albert Rose is the most recent, but he's not alone."

Sam looked blankly at Oscar Sampson.

"I'm trying to stop them," the elder lawyer said. "Do you have the stomach to become a double agent, and help me?"

Nine

The little red light on the Fish Fone started flashing, and wouldn't stop. So far, there were five text messages from Robert, clearly fronting for the Matriarchs. They had apparently made a collective decision to pile on, perhaps to reinforce to their new associate that, although he was accompanying the old man, it was the middle-aged women running the firm. And Robert was lazy. He just hit the "forward" button on each of their inquiries, dumping them on Sam. *Is this the same guy who was giving me the lowdown on the Matriarchs?* Sam wondered. *Now he's just forwarding their e-mails?*

Matriarch Connie, Director of Legal Recruiting, who made the original offer for Sam to join the Big Fish, was up first. She started with some of the banter they'd exchanged during the interview process. Connie was a Broadway theatre fan, and had just seen the latest hit show, a British West End import which was now impossible to get tickets to. It was an effective reminder that loyal soldiers at Fishbein, Schindler, Rose and Sampson would have their cultural needs met, not to mention the best seats in the house.

"Please extend my thanks to Connie," Sam formally texted back to Robert, assuming he would then pass it along. "She'll be interested to know the theatre offerings in downtown Chicago tend towards the touring companies of everything she saw three years ago in New York." Not that Sam had a spare moment to see any of the terrific productions among the Chicago-based theatres, which would probably be transferred to Broadway on their own cycle next year.

Matriarch Carol was second to bat. Carol handled Fishbein's finances, no small matter for a multi-billion-dollar company. She probably had most of the big stuff delegated to outside investment advisors who could produce detailed reports to satisfy the many partners with financial services expertise. As long as they delivered returns at or above the industry norm, Carol left them alone. It was just one base she covered for the Matriarchs.

The more important investments were the new associates like Sam. He had been brought into the fold a little sooner than Carol would have liked, but it's what seemed to mollify both Laura and Oscar. Her role for now would be to sweeten the pot.

"Since Sam is now working with Oscar in Chicago, we'll be holding a lot of his investment and retirement paperwork," she texted in an e-mail immediately forwarded by Robert. "Please reassure him, in case he asks, that we're already starting to put money away in an account for him. We can review the details once he gets closer to vesting." Translated, that meant the Matriarchs held the purse strings both on payroll and retirement. Sam knew what it also meant: *the package will be even larger than the generous starting pay, and the real price for all this largesse was loyalty – to the Matriarchs.*

Sam hadn't had any real contact with Carol, except to compliment her on her trendy eyewear the one time they had met during his associate summer. Red and turquoise-shell glasses, which probably cost a small fortune.

"Please extend my thanks to Carol. I appreciate having someone like her managing my retirement portfolio." Sam wanted to imply that he liked his job, including the sudden travel, and planned to make his career with Fishbein, Schindler,

Rose and Sampson. *Even if three founding partners are dead and the fourth just asked me to go undercover,* he thought.

Matriarch Mindy was the Director of Case Management. Her job was similar to that of a military leader in charge of several platoons. She charted the legal personnel needs of all the major clients, and made sure there were enough partners, associates, paralegals, assistants and secretaries among the national and offshore offices to handle the work.

Keeping the internal staff fully billable was her obvious priority. For the overflow, Mindy also had contract lawyers, paralegals and assistants in annex offices. The overflow workers got a good hourly rate, but none of the package benefits of Fishbein full-time staff.

"DeSantis Industries has been such an integral part of our growth," said her forwarded text. "The anticipated restructuring could be a very labor-intensive endeavor."

Sam had to laugh at that one. Mindy HOPED the bust-up of DeSantis would be labor-intensive. Hoped it would involve lots and lots of squabbling lawyers, contested motions, hearings before various judges. All billed by the hour, of course. *Lawyers, like lions, always feed first,* Sam thought.

"Please extend my thanks to Mindy," Sam began, knowing he could sound as rote and boring as he needed to in this job. "Oscar is giving me a solid sense of the history, and I look forward to making a contribution."

The next Matriarch note was a surprise, this one from Matriarch Sarah, Fishbein's Director of Marketing and Business Development. The newest Matriarch, and Robert's personal friend. In the forwarded e-mail, she muttered something about Oscar's leadership in various facets of M&A law, and how she hoped time might permit his review of the various seminar speaking and media interview "opportunities" she had forwarded to him.

Sarah was definitely at the bottom of the Matriarch hierarchy. Fishbein's business grew on the success of its lawyers. Matriarch

Sarah's job was mostly to decline the various time-wasting inquiries from seminar producers and legal bloggers. Sam wondered if she had been promoted because of prowess in some other arena.

"Please extend my thanks to Sarah," Sam said. "I look forward to working with her." *Who is she?* Sam thought.

Finally, the Matriarch e-mail series ended with the leader of the pack. Laura's question was simple, but icily prescient of all the activities in Chicago. "How is Oscar holding up under the strain?" she asked.

"Please extend my thanks to Laura for this assignment," Sam said, with as much diplomacy as he could muster. "I'm mindful that Oscar is managing a client relationship going back decades. I'm confident I can bring value to the next chapter." *Value?* Sam thought. *Where did I come up with that?*

Five messages from five piling-on Matriarchs wasn't all Sam would have to consider as he weighed the game-changing question from Oscar Sampson. The women whose opinions he *had* learned to respect also weighed in.

Jane Chapnick had kept a respectful distance from her Columbia academic perch since Sam defected to Fishbein, Schindler, Rose and Sampson. She never berated him for picking the Big Fish over Mothers Need Lawyers. She had made her own deal with money years ago, when she walked away from corporate law herself. On an Ivy League clinical law professor's salary, she could still afford nice clothes. She just didn't like to wear them every day, the way the Matriarchs did. She could also dress down, the way her students did.

The need for good public interest attorneys would never go away, Jane reassured herself, *and sometimes new corporate lawyers bail once they figured out just how dreary their everyday lives could become. After they made some money. After they discovered that they could* **make** *money, but not* **save** *money.*

Jane Chapnick was also kind of a wiseass, which Sam found to be among her most endearing qualities. "Made your first million yet?" her text asked, quickly followed more practically by, "Can I count on you to coordinate the Fishbein table at our autumn benefit?"

"Getting slammed right now," was the quickest reply Sam could think of that would both not lie but not volunteer uncomfortable information. He followed it with a quick, "of course I'll help."

The seventh flashing light on his Fish Fone was an incoming call, not a text. "Theresa" said the caller ID. Sam pressed the green button.

"Hey, how's the patient?"

"Well, she's okay. Lot of doctors, lots of nurses, lots of chemo, but balanced by terrific hospital cuisine and my always-sunny disposition. And a hovering mother, who I just sent down to the cafeteria to give us both a break."

"What do the doctors say?"

"They say they have to bring my whole immune system down to knock out the leukemia. It's like the damned breast cancer all over again, but even worse on the horror scale. I can't sleep without pills, and I throw up all the time because of the pills. Then there's the IVs. I feel like a pin cushion. I don't want to talk about it. I hear you're in Chicago?"

"Yeah, good news and bad news. Good news is I'm working with one of the firm's giants on a huge project. Bad news is I'm working with one of the firm's giants on a huge project."

"Great, you're mastering lawyer double-speak. How's the new wardrobe holding up?"

"Well, I haven't spilled anything on myself, always a plus. And, when you're out of town, they pick up your dry cleaning and laundry from your hotel room and deliver it back. I am the classiest, and cleanest, I've ever been."

"How do your suits compare to the partners and clients?"

"Mine are nice, theirs are nicer."

"That's perfect, you're new. We'll maintain that tone for

now," said his uncompensated wardrobe and professional style consultant.

"Okay, I gotta go. Take care of Mom."

"What's up with her? She actually knows one of the partners you're working with?"

"Yeah, neither will tell me the details, but I'll figure it out."

"Well, keep me posted. I'll see if I can pump her for more information. I can use the distraction."

"I've got distraction to spare. Take care."

Sam's decision had already pretty much formed in his head, but there was still time for one more call from a powerful woman. In Sandi's case, she was also the most attractive.

"Well, if it isn't the lovely lady in the next cube," he said. "What are you up to?"

"I'm up to my neck in DeSantis files," she said. "This is going to be the mother of all bankruptcies. More associates are being added every day."

"Well, I've somehow ended up in the thick of it," Sam said. "I'm sitting in Chicago where it was born, and you're in New York, where it will die."

"Robert is watching everyone like a mother hen. He says this is the top priority for the firm, and the Matriarchs keep hovering, wondering if anyone other than Robert has heard from you."

"What are they up to?"

Sandi's next line clinched it for Sam: "It's probably way too early in our professional relationship to trust you with this, but my gut says something's wrong. The DeSantis files are never out of Robert's sight. He's running back and forth to the Matriarchs all the time, lots of closed-door meetings. They send you to Chicago to baby-sit Oscar Sampson, while we're preparing to cut his Chicago baby into pieces."

"We think a lot alike," Sam said.

"There's one more thing," Sandi added.

"Robert asked you out," Sam said, and held his breath.

"Oh, God, no," Sandi said quickly. "Thank God, no."

"Just checking," Sam said, surprised at himself for being this ballsy around an attractive woman. His typical response was to clam up and shut down. Like many men, Sam was better at business than flirting.

"So, what?" he asked.

"I just saw something kind of weird," Sandi said.

"What was it?"

"I was in my cube, and saw Matriarch Sarah come down to Robert's office."

"Aren't they friends? That's what he said."

"Who knows? What was doubly weird was what she said."

"Tell me," Sam said.

"She said, 'Albert Rose gone!' to which he replied 'and our Miss Sarah promoted!' And then they high-fived each other'"

"Okay, that is doubly weird," Sam said.

"Sarah and Robert seem to have become allies," Sandi concluded.

"Sounds like it," said Sam. "We'll have to keep an eye on them."

"And the other eye on our backs," Sandi said. "This place is full of vipers."

"Well, right now, they're also signing our paychecks," Sam said.

"Agreed," Sandi said. "I gotta go."

"Okay," Sam said. "Let's stay in touch."

"One more thing," Sandi said, "Take care of yourself. We miss you."

"You mean you miss me?" Sam joked.

"Bye, Sam," Sandi said, hanging up.

Sam's final call of the day was to his Mom's cell phone. He didn't want to talk; he just wanted to leave a message. She was probably still inside the hospital's basement cafeteria.

"Hi, it's me. I don't know everything that's going on, but I know enough to pick sides. Tell your friend Oscar I'm in. He'd better have been your boyfriend *before* Dad."

Ten

Matriarch Laura always wore the same outfit on the days she fired Fishbein employees. A slate blue power suit, the color psychologists say has a calming effect. Everyone who spent any time around Laura knew better. Slate blue had the power to terrify at Fishbein, Schindler, Rose and Sampson.

This time, there would be more than one firing. A package deal. And these firings would serve multiple purposes. Remove problem employees, and send a message to new employees at a critical time.

Laura was a woman comforted by routine, and along with her slate blue power suit, she needed validation from her protégés. The other Matriarchs got just a little advance warning – a heads-up on their Fish Fones to meet Laura for breakfast at 8:30 a.m. The women with the matching large-stoned rings were already on board, of course. Laura's tactics were always brilliant, if at times harsh.

"Is the paperwork ready?" asked Laura at breakfast.

"We're good to go," said Matriarch Mindy. The DeSantis restructuring was an area of special concern these days, and Laura had deputized Mindy to assist with today's hatchet job. Mindy knew Laura would wear her slate blue suit, so she chose a cream-colored ensemble just delivered by Susan from Saks.

"We have draft letters of employment termination, benefit overviews, and standard release forms," Mindy said. "For both of them."

"Excellent. Start with Sandi."

Robert was watching Sandi's cubicle, waiting for her phone to ring. He'd witnessed this process before. He liked Sandi, and he liked the wiseass kid in the next cubicle, Sam. But no one stayed at Fishbein just because they were liked. There was too much money involved. Not to mention the departing founding partners.

Sandi's phone rang at 9:02 a.m. This operation was to follow a precise script, hammered out over time with employment law experts to minimize the firm's exposure. "Hi, Sandi, it's Mindy. Do you have time to join me for a few minutes in the small conference room?"

"Of course," said a surprised Sandi. "I'll be right there."

Sandi looked up at Robert across the hall, who had stationed himself at the entry to his window office. He simply motioned for her to go.

Sandi then felt the fear. *Why am I being summoned by one of the Matriarchs? What have I done? What could possibly have happened that would get me in trouble so soon?* As her mind fogged with questions and doubt, the heel of her shoe caught in the thick carpet, and she tripped. It took all her strength just to maintain her balance as she pushed through the glass door and onto the elevator.

Matriarch Mindy could almost smell Sandi's fear as the young lawyer entered the windowless conference room. Instilling fear was part of the process. The Matriarchs would get more information this way, and send a not-so-subtle power message to everyone who would hear of this meeting later.

"Hi, Sandi, how are you today?" Mindy began. "Laura Henderson is joining us on the speaker phone."

"I'm fine, thanks," Sandi said, knowing she was not in for a fair fight, and thinking she was about to be fired.

"Sandi, as you know, the DeSantis restructuring is very important to us," said Matriarch Laura, her voice projected through the speaker phone. Laura was in her office two flights away, multi-tasking on her e-mail. Appearing via speakerphone just heightened the drama.

"I know it is," Sandi said. "Is there a problem, something I can help with?" Sandi still had no idea why she was summoned, her level of personal risk, or where all of this was headed.

It was Mindy's turn to jump in. "This is a delicate matter, and involves a primary client of the firm."

Laura added, "And we're concerned about our internal security related to this complicated matter. We need to ask you a few questions about the professionalism of your colleagues."

Sandi could feel a slight tremor in her right hand. Pure fear. She instinctively drew her hands together and looked straight into Mindy's eyes. Something told her to focus on the person in the room, not the speakerphone.

"I had no idea there was a problem," Sandi said, which was true. All she'd done so far was gut through DeSantis files, and keep tabs on Sam in Chicago.

"We're concerned about the integrity of our records, especially the securities filings over the years of DeSantis and its subsidiaries." The voice was Laura's, via the speakerphone, but Sandi kept looking at Mindy's face for clues. It was a wise strategic choice on Sandi's part, since she could see that Mindy was following Laura's script, and Mindy kept looking down at the speakerphone instead of maintaining eye contact with Sandi. Laura was known as the First Matriarch for good reason. If the Matriarchs were a pack of she-lions, Laura was the undisputed leader of the pack.

"Sandi, from your desk you can see both Anthony Daniels and Kenya Washington, isn't that correct?" Laura asked.

"Yes, they're both within a couple of cubicles," Sandi replied, suddenly flashing on one of the evidence-versus-hearsay exercises from law school.

"And have you ever seen Anthony and Kenya handling any files or electronic records from the DeSantis matter?"

"Of course, they're both secretaries working with us. They handle files all day."

"Have you heard Anthony and Kenya discussing the case?"

"I don't recall any specific conversations, but it's our main project, so I'm sure it's been discussed."

"And have you personally witnessed Anthony or Kenya handling any outgoing faxes on the DeSantis matter?"

"I have not personally witnessed them at the fax machine, which is in a separate room, but I would assume they both fax documents all the time. Again, the DeSantis case is our primary project."

"Yes, and as you probably know, Anthony and Kenya have both been with us for a number of years as team members on a number of sensitive projects."

"Is there a connection, or some suggestion of impropriety on their part?" Sandi asked, wondering if Mindy would have any additional lines in this unfolding drama.

"I'm afraid so," said the First Matriarch. "Thanks for taking the time to talk with us this morning. We'll get back to you if we need anything else."

"Thanks, Sandi. Have a great day," said Mindy, ushering Sandi out the door.

Sandi needed some time to process what had just happened, and whether her words were about to be used against the two people who shared her office floor. She was also determined not to trip again as she made her way back to the elevator.

The answers came quickly enough. Anthony and Kenya were delivered by Robert to Mindy's waiting conference room, and a short time later were escorted by security officers out the door.

Eleven

The drive between Chicago and Milwaukee doesn't take very long, especially if you pick up a rental car first thing in the morning, avoid the traffic, and drive at the high end of the acceptable speed range – six, but not seven, miles per hour over the posted limit. Oscar Sampson understood Sam's desire for a quick trip home, and they both thought that with the Fish Fone, no one back in New York would be the wiser. Oscar would hold down the fort in Chicago.

Theresa was feeling better, she'd said. She was still in the hospital, still enduring the chemo and radiation typical after a recent leukemia diagnosis, but the nausea and vomiting had eased up.

The one who was feeling nauseous this time was Sam. It was probably the additive effect of the time with Oscar Sampson, all the Matriarchs piling on, plus the telephone conversation with Sandi. She'd called to tell him about the Matriarch's latest move.

"Tell me again what happened," he'd said.

"There's not that much to tell. I was summoned to a little interrogation chamber, asked a couple of perfunctory questions about two of the most junior secretaries, then they were dismissed."

Sam would ask Oscar about it later, but figured the two

secretaries had been feeding information at Oscar's request to DeSantis in Chicago. *Probably just answering questions as they were phoned in,* Sam thought. *Robert was always hovering, and probably saw the outgoing faxes. He passed the valuable tidbit along to Sarah, knowing it would go further up the chain. The Matriarchs decided to plug the leak. Any effect of the dismissals on the secretaries' personal lives was acceptable collateral damage. Human pawns in a larger chess game.*

"I think the decision to sack them was made before you entered the room," Sam said.

"Agreed. So why bring me into it?"

"Probably to scare you, and maybe to see if they can trust you to be a team player – on *their* team." Sam was tempted to say more, much more, but he didn't know Sandi well enough to trust her with everything he knew. He also wondered how much risk they had both just assumed, since their conversation had been between two Fish Fones. Would the Matriarchs have any reason to be monitoring their cell phones?

Sam decided against acting any more paranoid than he already was, at least for now.

"So, how are you doing with the old men in Chicago?" Sandi asked.

"Well, I think we both have evidence that the DeSantis restructuring is far more complicated than we thought," he said. "Listen, I appreciate you telling me all this. Can I fill you in on my side later? And maybe we should start using our personal cell phones when we talk?"

"Absolutely," Sandi said. "I should get back to my desk before Robert notices I'm gone. I just had to tell someone about this."

"I'm glad you picked me," Sam said, and meant it.

Once he arrived at the cancer ward, Sam washed his hands in the special sink, and donned the required white mask before entering his sister's room. It was going to be tough to interrogate his mother with both of them wearing masks, and with the leukemia patient in the bed between them.

Whatever anger Sam felt towards his mother melted as soon as he looked at Theresa. The nausea may have eased, but she looked noticeably worse than the last time. Maybe it was the fluorescent lighting in the room, but she looked pale and drawn. And he could instantly tell that his Mom's concern was right in this room, not with anything happening at the Chicago or New York offices of Fishbein, Schindler, Rose and Sampson.

Sam knew he wasn't allowed to hug his sister, because that would risk infection to her now very compromised immune system. So he was relieved when his Mom made the first move to speak.

"Listen, I'm sorry. Not telling you that I knew Oscar was a mistake."

Theresa immediately pounced on the chance to take the focus away from her leukemia and onto something – anything – else. "So tell us the Oscar Sampson story."

"There isn't that much of a story," said Barbara Mitcham.

"Whatever you've got will be more entertaining than what I've got," said Theresa.

Mrs. Mitcham sighed, and started to speak. "Oscar Sampson was a senior. Your dad was a sophomore. I was a freshman. Most of the boys in my high school were creeps. Oscar and your Dad were not. They were classy, they were friendly, and they were fun."

"So you were friends," Sam said.

"Well, at the start Oscar and your Dad were friends. Oscar sort of set us up. Your Dad was too shy to approach me himself."

"Oscar was the matchmaker?" Sam and Theresa asked, in unison.

"I guess, but remember, this was high school. We were all just fumbling around. Talking by the hallway lockers on the way from classes to lunch. One day, Oscar told me Larry Mitcham wanted to ask me to a dance, but wouldn't unless he knew I'd say yes."

"Oscar arranged the deals, even back in high school." Sam was smiling underneath his mask. Theresa managed a small chuckle herself.

"Well, that's a little crude, but yes, Oscar did arrange the deal."

"And then what?" Sam asked.

"Larry and I hit it off. We started dating. We were sort of together ever since."

"And Oscar?"

"Well, Oscar was around that year, but then he graduated, breezed through college, and headed off to law school. He was an ambitious guy and wanted to make a name for himself. He ended up in New York. We stayed in Wisconsin."

"And you stayed in touch," Theresa said.

"Sure, we stayed in touch," Barbara Mitcham said, adjusting her face mask. She was not comfortable being interviewed by her children, one of them a just-minted lawyer. "Sometimes we talked on the phone. Some years, especially when Oscar was building the law firm, it went down to just the annual Christmas card."

Theresa seemed satisfied. Sam knew there was more – perhaps it was all those hours in law school, learning to look at the underside of every argument.

"When your Dad had the strokes and was so sick, Oscar always called to check in. When he passed away, Oscar called all the time, just to make sure I was OK."

"So, Dad died five years ago. What's your contact with Oscar been like since then?" Sam asked, earning the glare his Mom shot at him.

"Listen, young man, I'm under no obligation to tell you everything about my personal life."

"No, you're not," Theresa said. "I'm still in shock that you have a personal life that's so much more interesting than mine."

"Actually, our talks became less and less frequent the past

couple of years," their Mom said. "But he did call when he learned you were part of the new associate class at Fishbein. He wanted to make sure it was you."

"Mom, I think he's in a whole lot of trouble," Sam said.

"Yeah, I get that part. Can you help him?"

"I'm going to give it a shot," Sam Mitcham said to his mother, looking down at the cancer ward's linoleum floor. He wasn't sure where the feeling was coming from, but he had an acute sense that his mother wasn't telling everything she knew about Oscar Sampson. And for now, he had pushed as hard as he could. After all, Barbara Mitcham was *his* Matriarch.

Twelve

This time, on the plane between Chicago and New York, Oscar Sampson didn't try to dodge a conversation with Sam by taking a nap. He was eager to talk to his new junior partner.

Like the dealmaker he was, Oscar Sampson knew when to acknowledge the 800-pound gorilla in the room, or in this case, the first class cabin.

"Not sure who you can trust, right? Including your own mother, who has been the one person you've implicitly trusted your whole life."

"You nailed that one, Oscar," said Sam, who was now clearly past the thought of referring to the senior partner as "sir" or "Mr. Sampson."

"Where do you want me to start? The relationship with your parents, my dead partners, the Matriarchs, or my imploding client?"

"I'm assuming you've talked with my mother since I met with her. Your stories will probably line up perfectly."

"Barbara was right; you're not very respectful around your elders."

"Right now my elders appear to be responsible for a huge and dangerous shift in my career trajectory. I'm not sure they deserve my respect. What they've mostly got is my concern."

"Lighten up, Sam. That attitude will get you nowhere. First off, the family history is true. I met your parents in high school. I set them up on their first date. We've kept in touch over the years, and I tried to be there for Barbara when Larry died. And, by the way, I'm very sorry about Theresa. She's a strong girl, and if anyone can pull through leukemia on top of breast cancer, it's her."

"That's all?" Sam asked.

"What else could there be?"

"Excuse me if I get the sense that both you and Mom aren't lying, but also aren't volunteering information."

"Tell me what's on your mind."

"Did Mom know Fishbein, Schindler, or Rose?"

"No"

"Does Mom know Peter DeSantis?"

"She's never met him, so far as I know."

"Does Mom know the Matriarchs?"

"She knows of them, but hasn't dealt with them directly."

"This is not increasing my comfort level, Oscar."

"Yes, I can tell."

Oscar Sampson knew it was time to recalibrate his argument for him to have any chance of winning Sam over to his side. "Why don't we put that aside for now, and talk about the DeSantis restructuring?" he asked.

"Funny how it's easier to talk about business than our personal lives," Sam said.

"Of course it is," Oscar said. "We get a lot more training in business."

On the business of DeSantis Industries, they found common ground, and much for Sam to learn. Plus, Sam had information to share. He told Oscar about Sandi, about Robert, and about the two unfortunate secretaries who got sacked.

In the midst of his updates, Sam saw an opportunity to go on the offensive. "It doesn't say good things about your position at the firm that you weren't able to protect two secretaries supplying you with information from New York headquarters," he charged.

"Rub my nose in it if you want to, kid. I guess you're entitled. But here's another way to look at it: doesn't this provide evidence that I genuinely need the help of someone like you, even though you're brand new to most of this? And, by the way, I'm genuinely sorry about Anthony and Kenya. They won't have any trouble finding other jobs. I'll provide sterling references."

Over the years, Oscar had developed more of a talent for swallowing bad news than Sam currently possessed. Oscar Sampson had just received confirmation that two junior soldiers were taken out by the Matriarchs. His response was to shrug his shoulders, and immediately move on. Sam thought that if Oscar represented the qualities of a successful corporate lawyer, he might not have the stomach for it.

Or, maybe he did. A whole line of questions popped into Sam's head. He wanted to know about the deceased Fishbein, Schindler, and Rose. The fourth named partner, who was still very much alive, anticipated the questions.

"To begin with, we were partners, but we weren't friends," Oscar began. "Fishbein was a little man. Not just little in stature, though the whole Napoleon Complex thing was probably true in his case. He was little as a person, too. Efficient and gracious on the outside, mean on the inside. That's why he and Laura got along so well."

"But brilliant in court, and he anticipated the waves of corporate mergers," said Sam.

"Well, if I do say so myself, we were all kind of brilliant in practice. And, all of us had the one other necessary ingredient: we were ambitious, maybe even greedy. We saw opportunities where no one else did, doing the business no one else wanted."

"Why did you allow Laura to build up the whole Matriarch

thing?"

"Why not? Say what you will about her methods, and all the rumors, but she's been a completely efficient businesswoman. No one developed a more successful business model. Our profits per partner always led the pack. We did the lawyering, built the client base, kept the new clients coming in. She handled everything else."

"With a high body count, at least if you count founding partners."

"Sam, you don't know what you're talking about. I know you're still pissed off at me and your mother, but there's a big difference between aggressive business tactics and whatever those silly legal blogs are saying about Albert Rose's death."

Sam decided it was time to accept the flight attendant's latest offer of alcoholic beverages. Vodka martinis, free in the first class cabin. In real glasses, not plastic like they had in coach. More conducive to a high-class argument.

After a few sips, Sam continued his exploration of Oscar's professional past.

"So what happened to Fishbein?"

"Morris was 82. He'd ignored his high blood pressure for years. Laura didn't have anything to do with it. She worshipped him."

"Next came Schindler," Sam said. "Died in 2003 at the age of 66."

"No one thought to question it," Oscar said. "He was starting to turn on Laura and her Matriarchs, but he was kind of a mess all by himself. He drank like a fish, smoked like a chimney, cheated on his wife – the typical descent. He was in the middle of a huge case. A ton of pressure. He may not have died of natural causes, but no one found a smoking gun."

"Then Albert Rose," Sam said. "Age 64."

"Yeah, I know," said Oscar. "I read the headlines too. 'Albert Rose – Was His Corner Office a Deathtrap?' And, to finish your line of reasoning, here's Oscar Sampson, still hanging on at 63. Just one year younger."

"Are you in personal danger?"

"Kid, I've already apologized to your mother for this. You and I are both in danger."

Thirteen

Sam barely made it through the door of his New York apartment before the phone rang. It was Sandi, offering to get together for pizza and an update on what was going on at the home office.

They met at John's Pizzeria, a place popular with Times Square tourists. It was in a giant old bank building in the West 40s, with one whole wall featuring a hand-painted mural depicting New York City scenes. The mural reminded Sam that he hadn't seen much of the City since he began the job at Fishbein. He knew that his life would have been more his own had he opted for Mothers Need Lawyers. But then, he wouldn't have met Sandi, and he'd barely be able to afford pizza.

Sandi, wearing another trendy outfit with a slit skirt, was much more interested in sharing work news than in eating. She told Sam to order whatever he wanted. Soon they were sharing a delicious thin-crust pie with cheese, Canadian bacon, and pepperoni. Sam grew up ordering the same combination in Wisconsin. Of course, in Wisconsin the pizza always came with ice-cold draft beer, which happily was also available at John's Pizzeria in New York.

"So, the Matriarchs cleared away a couple of secretaries who were actually responsive to requests from Chicago," Sam began, sipping his draft. "How did that go over?"

"Well, no one has heard from them since. And everyone else just put their heads down and went back to work. Their desks have already been filled with a couple of secretaries shifted over from another department. All requests from Chicago go to Robert, of course. No one will touch them."

"We're working in a factory," Sam said. He glanced at their Fish Fones, which they'd both placed on the table. You never knew when the red light would start flashing, indicating something needed by someone, and the young up-and-comers at Fishbein were always on call.

"Sure feels like a factory, maybe a factory farm," Sandi said. "This culling of the herd has clearly happened before. I'm sure the long-term staff are talking about it, but none of them know me well enough to trust me. And, since I was the one called in to the Matriarchs before the ax fell, some of the old-timers probably blame me for it."

"How about the other associates?" Sam asked.

"None of the other associates know anything, except to be a lot more careful than before with anything labeled 'DeSantis.'"

"And how is our good friend Robert?"

"Not a word. From what I can see, Robert is just funneling the work, guarding the files, and keeping out of the line of fire. That means doing whatever the Matriarchs tell him to do, especially Sarah."

"Have you seen them together lately?"

"Yeah, she stops down to his office a lot," Sandi said. "I haven't seen any more high-fiving; she just goes into his office and closes the door."

At that moment, the red light on Sandi's Fish Fone started to flash. It was a text message from Robert, asking about a document she had reviewed earlier in the day.

"Robert doesn't have a life," sighed Sandi. She typed a concise, respectful answer to the question, read it over three times like the lawyer she was, and hit *send*.

Sam's mind drifted while Sandi took care of Robert's pressing business. The draft beer he sipped was a long way from its Wisconsin brewery home, but traveled well. When Sandi finished, he steered back to the DeSantis restructuring at the Big Fish.

"I don't remember any case studies like this at my law school," Sam said. "How about yours?"

"No, but remember, I went to the also-ran second-tier school. I would think this kind of thing would be far more likely to come up in the Ivy League," Sandi joked. "How's your family?"

"My sister is doing okay, considering they're pouring toxic chemicals into her all day to get the leukemia into remission. My Mom is doing what moms do best at a time like this. She's hovering." Sam decided to not tell Sandi, at least not yet, about the connection between his Mom and Oscar Sampson. He didn't think he knew the true extent of their story himself.

But there was plenty to tell Sandi about Oscar and DeSantis Industries. She had read most of the history, had waded through many of the files, but hadn't seen the headquarters with the plush carpeting, dark wood, and reverential staff. She hadn't heard that Oscar and Peter DeSantis were old buddies who built a conglomerate together, with each new acquisition being toasted over cognac at Chicago's Mercantile Club. She didn't know that the spread of DeSantis Industries mirrored, and helped facilitate, the explosive growth of Fishbein, Schindler, Rose and Sampson. Sam regaled her with the surface details, but stopped short of saying everything he knew.

Sam wasn't ready to tell anyone else, even the beautiful co-worker sitting across from him in the restaurant booth, that he had agreed to become a double agent for Oscar Sampson.

It would've been nice to vent about the founding partner who coincidentally knew his Mom from high school, had stayed in touch all these years, and then apologized for putting them both in harm's way. It probably would've been psychologically healthy to say all that out loud. But Sam reflected the stereotype of Midwesterners – nice and friendly on the outside, a lot buried inside. Stereotypes are often based on observable fact.

The waiter stopped at their table, and Sam ordered another round of beers without asking Sandi. She didn't object.

Sam's Fish Fone started flashing red. It was Robert. A softball question about one of the documents Sam had read in Chicago. Sam was able to bat an answer back almost on pure instinct, but did think to have Sandi review it before he hit *send*.

"Do you think Robert is really back at the office right now, or just doing an off-hours drill with all his DeSantis associates?" Sandi asked.

"I bet it's just a little fire drill," Sam said. "You've got to wonder if it's just him, or him and Sarah, or what."

"Fear is a strong motivator. Maybe he's trying to anticipate what he thinks she wants … or what the other Matriarchs want."

"Well, here's one we both did read about in law school. Big corporate firms, like the one we have joined, pride themselves on 'breaking down walls' for their clients. Those walls come in all shapes and sizes, and at all times of the day and night. Associates hand over the keys to their youth, and in return they get buckets of money."

"What are you doing with yours?" Sandi asked.

"Well, first of all," Sam began, talking like a guy who was on his third beer. "The gross is amazing, but I never thought to calculate the net. Taxes add up here, especially when you factor in federal, plus State of New York, plus City of New York. Each one its own taxing entity. Associates take home a hell of a lot more in Chicago."

"How about rent?"

"Exactly, higher here than anywhere else in the Western Hemisphere. New York City may be the Capital of the World, but it charges really high dues."

"That sounds like a line you've used before."

"It is. But here's another one. We are lucky to have these concerns. We have luxury problems. No one's going hungry at this table." Sam glanced at the round metal pizza plate, which had come from an authentic brick pizza oven to their table. He grabbed the last slice.

"Perhaps you're a man of large appetites, just like the founders of our firm."

"Ambition isn't a bad thing," Sam said defensively. "And I'm not the only one who heard early on from the Matriarchs, promising more – much more – as a reward for faithful service."

"Yeah, I got that message too. Money as positive reinforcement; quite a carrot. You start to understand why a guy like Robert behaves the way he does, and jumps when they call."

At that moment, their Fish Fones began flashing simultaneously. A text message from Robert, asking Sam, Sandi, and all the DeSantis associates to be in by 7:30 a.m. for an important meeting.

They hustled to get the check and get home in time for a few hours sleep in preparation for an early morning at Fishbein, Schindler, Rose and Sampson. Like the Midwestern gentleman he was, Sam walked Sandi to the subway station, and waited until she was down the stairs before heading home to unpack and crash.

Fourteen

Sam was not a morning person. He didn't like to get up while it was still dark outside.

But if he had to be conscious and in the office by 7:30 a.m., there was no choice. Three beers the night before were not helping. Neither was the pot of coffee he'd just swallowed. He knew he had to make it on time, be present and accounted for, and ready for anything. Fire drill.

Matriarch Mindy, Director of Case Management, had positioned herself at the head of the conference room. First Matriarch Laura was there to lend an air of importance to the occasion, as were the other Matriarchs, standing as a pack against the wall. They were wearing their typical conservative power suits, with modest jewelry. All five wore their matching giant blue diamond rings, and Matriarch Carol sported her trendy eye glasses. In a word, they looked formidable. And, as always, united behind Laura. Robert sat mute, nodding along whenever a Matriarch glanced in his direction.

"Thanks for joining us this morning," Mindy began. "We'll be here for just a few minutes, then everyone can get back to work on behalf of our clients." She forced a tiny smile.

"We're concerned about some of the conduct we've witnessed lately, and we know that most of the problems are attributable to the relative youth of our DeSantis team."

The team is youthful, Sam thought, *because no one lasts too long in the service of DeSantis Industries. Or on the wrong side of the Matriarchs.*

"For the sake of efficiency, I've compiled a short list of reminders," Mindy said. The recent law school grads instinctively prepared to take notes.

"First, everyone was trained as a law student to write with precision and clarity. Our document proofreaders have reported an error rate as high as one per page. And not just typos. Errors in syntax, poor use of legal terminology. Embarrassing, really." The Matriarchs nodded in unison.

Sam looked at Sandi, then glanced at Robert. *Wasn't editing Robert's responsibility?* For his part, Robert was simply nodding. He did seem to look at Sarah more than he did at the other Matriarchs.

"Next, some in this room have not yet mastered our timekeeping system, which is our bread and butter. You are required to account for every 10 minutes of your billable time. On a large account like DeSantis, you must rigorously log your time by the proper account sub-code. If you have any questions, please be sure to contact Robert."

Robert nodded again, first in the direction of the Matriarchs, then at his impressionable crop of first-year associates.

"Third on my list, professional conduct and attire. We expect that everyone dress appropriately and professionally in this office. We've been especially concerned about the length of hemlines and the height of heels." Sandi was probably the smartest dresser in the office, though at this moment she was painfully aware that her skirt was shorter than the Matriarchs' power suits. And her heels were higher. And she looked great in both. And that was probably the point.

"Let me pause in case anyone has questions or is unclear on any point," said Mindy. *What was there to ask?* the new associates wondered.

"Sandi, Denise, and Lisa, are you hearing me about appropriate work attire?" Mindy added. Sandi, Denise and Lisa, the most stylish of the new associates, suddenly looked ashen. They glanced at each other, and then looked down, nodding.

"Mindy, thank you for bringing these matters to our attention," interjected Matriarch Laura, who started walking slowly towards the door. "Again, everyone, I appreciate your help, and know we'll take care of any problems immediately." She looked at her Fish Fone, which of course was flashing with many more pressing items, and left the room.

The Director of Case Management pushed on with her list. "Okay, now, let's talk about security. Everyone is required to swipe in at the front desk, at the elevators, and at the entrance to this unit. If you come in with someone else, you must both swipe. I've been looking at the security printouts, and it appears that we're not being consistent."

Then, Mindy's remarks on ID card swiping turned into another specific swipe at the junior women. "I know it's probably more fashionable not to fasten a card to your skirt or pants suit, especially if you're just going to the cafeteria or ladies room. But it's really necessary on an important case like this, and also reflects our internal camaraderie as employees of Fishbein, Schindler, Rose and Sampson. Wear it with pride."

Sandi glared at Sam as if to say, "Is she for real?" The faces of the other members of the DeSantis team, especially the young women attorneys, looked blank.

Sam thought he detected subtle smiles on the faces of the other Matriarchs as they, one by one, noticed their Fish Fones were flashing, and exited the conference room. It was kind of like watching the mean girls leaving the playground after they'd destroyed the vulnerable new girl. Except these were grown-up women, in the office of a billion-dollar business.

But Mindy wasn't done yet. She had one more.

"Our security concerns aren't limited to ID cards, unfortunately," she said. "As you know, we've lost a couple of our colleagues recently."

Lost a couple of colleagues? thought Sam. Everyone knew they had been sacked.

"Every outgoing fax must be coded and a confirmation receipt filed," Mindy said. "On this, we can really tolerate no exceptions."

Sam looked around the room. The new associates had probably entered this meeting thinking they would be discussing the meat of the DeSantis restructuring. The intricate and confidential efforts the team was undertaking to assist this valuable client at its most difficult time. Instead, they had been told to improve their embarrassing legal writing, bill every available second, dress worse than the Matriarchs, and always swipe. Oh, and to watch those faxes, because anyone sending anything to Oscar Sampson or Peter DeSantis in Chicago will be out of a job.

And, with ruthless precision, the Matriarchs had seeded the team with fear and insecurity. Sam wondered how many times they'd used these tactics with other teams on other partners' big projects.

"Thanks again, everyone," Mindy said, ending the meeting. "If you have any questions, please do not hesitate to contact me or any of your senior managers." Mindy then glanced at her blinking Fish Fone, and started reading e-mails and walking away at the same time. She was wearing sensible low heels, so there was no risk that she'd trip on the carpet. There was also no risk that anyone would ever approach her with a follow-up question on the almost surreal content of this meeting.

Robert was left in the conference room, surrounded by his team of associates. If they were looking to him for reassurance after the Matriarchs power play, they were looking to the wrong guy. "Okay," he said. "Let's keep all of that in mind. I'll be bringing by more materials for each of you later today."

Apparently dismissed, Sam, Sandi and the other newbies filed back in the direction of their cubicles.

Sam knew his female colleagues would start wearing their

most conservative outfits, and a few would probably have to go shopping wherever dour women got their clothes. No more slit skirts, that was for sure. He'd have a good story for his next phone call with Theresa, who'd arranged Sam's wardrobe so he'd fit in at Fishbein, Schindler, Rose and Sampson.

It's easier for young men to suit up than young women, she'd remind him. And it would be extra tough for women who happened to be younger and prettier than the Matriarchs.

As soon as they could, Sandi and the other young women ducked off the path to their cubicles and headed as a small pack of their own to the nearest ladies room. Having just been attacked by older women, they did not seek comfort from Sam or the other young men. Their only solace at that moment was to be together, hoping that no one saw their tears.

Fifteen

Oscar Sampson seemed truly saddened when Sam told him about the Matriarchs' efforts to terrorize the DeSantis team. Sam was right; the Matriarchs had done this drill before.

"You can't do anything about it?" Sam asked. Seeing Sandi and the other young women crying was enough to motivate Sam to risk a trip upstairs to Oscar's corner office.

"Give me a little credit, kid," said the remaining founding partner. "I may be on my last lap here, but I still have a few moves left in me. And, I'm not without friends at this firm."

Oscar Sampson could be as cryptic with information as Barbara Mitcham. Sam had been wondering a lot lately what moves Oscar might be contemplating.

Oscar's contemplation was done in luxurious surroundings. His corner office at Fishbein was similar to Matriarch Laura's – large, furnished in the same sort of dark woods Sam remembered from the office of Peter DeSantis in Chicago, and with amazing views of Lower Manhattan. Sam could make out the Statue of Liberty from this perch, just as he had from Laura's office. Oscar and Laura were in opposite corners, with overlapping views looking south. Sam wondered what the rental rates were for prime New York City office space like this.

Sam didn't know how careful to be in Oscar's office. He had, after all, been recruited by Oscar to be some sort of double agent, but the details hadn't been specified. Oscar didn't use a Fish Fone, and didn't communicate by e-mail. Were their conversations in his corner office being recorded by the Matriarchs? Sam figured if Laura and her minions were monitoring the ID swipe-ins of DeSantis associates, they wouldn't be above other forms of spying. *Or they could be up to much worse,* Sam thought, remembering the high-five Sandi reported between Sarah and Robert.

Oscar didn't seem too worried. Or maybe all those years of corporate negotiation had taught him how to keep a poker face.

"What's the deal with the girl?" Oscar asked.

"You mean Sandi?"

"Yeah. Too bad we won't be seeing any of her attractive outfits for awhile. Leave it to Laura to ruin the scenery." Sam had to admit, for a 63-year-old, Oscar hadn't lost his keen powers of observation.

Oscar pressed on. "What have you told her?"

"She knows I went with you to Chicago. She's read a lot of the DeSantis paperwork. We're becoming friends. I trust her. She knows my sister is sick."

"How is the family in Milwaukee?" asked Oscar, as if he didn't have a personal connection.

"Mom's fine, Theresa thinks a good day is one which doesn't include vomiting."

"You're related to strong women, kid," said Oscar. "That's a good thing. And, sounds as though you might have a good prospect there in your co-worker."

"Right," Sam said, not really interested in Oscar's take on his dating prospects. "So what's next on our plate?"

"Let's get out of here for awhile."

"Robert would notice my absence," Sam said.

"We can deal with people like Robert," Oscar said. "Don't get distracted by the little things."

Midtown New York is filled with restaurants where men like Oscar go for lunch. Some are designed to allow business people of Oscar Sampson's stature the opportunity to meet and greet. Some are built to facilitate private conversations. For this occasion, Oscar preferred the latter.

Billy's Grill was a lot like Chicago's Mercantile Club. This was probably where Oscar and Peter DeSantis went for lunch in New York. Billy's had been around a long time, and so had its staff. Oscar didn't need a reservation. He and his young charge were warmly greeted at the door, and taken to a private table in a corner.

"The usual, Mr. Sampson?" asked the waiter who had to be about Oscar's age, if not older.

"Yes, thank you, Frank. Sam, martini for you as well?"

The libations appeared almost instantly, in chilled glasses with just a hint of ice floating next to the olives and cocktail onions. They knew how to make a martini at Billy's Grill.

Sam thought of Sandi and the other associates back at the Big Fish. They were either grabbing something at the Fishbein cafeteria, or more likely bringing sandwiches back to their cubicles. Being with Oscar did have its creature comforts.

The steaks came next. Sam didn't recall being shown a menu, or being asked what he'd like to eat. The Billy's Grill staff made the correct calculation that if the young suit was drinking with Oscar Sampson, he'd enjoy the same filet mignon. Medium rare. A few side dishes. Refills on the martinis as needed.

After the second martini, Oscar decided it was time to talk business.

"Tell me about the DeSantis team, and the work they're doing."

"Don't you already know most of it? You built the company, after all."

"I know a lot of the history. The Matriarchs are keeping me in the dark, to the extent possible, on the dismantling operation."

"What faxes were the sacked secretaries trying to send to you in Chicago?"

"Executive compensation reports – what Peter DeSantis was getting paid, and how much he was paying managers at the subsidiaries. How much money was going into offshore accounts."

"That's not information you already had access to?"

"I knew some of it, not all. I hadn't seen every filing. What else are the associates looking at?"

"Well, as you know, there's paper going back 20 years, but the team's effort is mostly focused on the past year or so, and why everything went south so fast."

"Go on, I'm listening," Oscar said, motioning for Frank to bring another martini.

"It's a cobweb," Sam said. "All of the mergers after Addison Trucking had complicated financing, and each one was built on top of the one before it. So we're breaking down each one of the post-Addison acquisitions – how it was arranged, who was involved, the securities filings, the regulatory reports, everything we can lay our hands on."

"That's a mountain of paper," Oscar said.

"Yes, it is. And along with the paper files, there are electronic records of e-mails, assurances made, and promises evidently kept," Sam said. "There were a lot of moves made to keep DeSantis Industries looking good on paper."

"How much have you seen on executive compensation?" Oscar asked.

"Not much," Sam replied. "There's the reporting of revenue allotted to management at existing and acquired companies, fees associated with each acquisition paid to consultants and counsel, that kind of thing. Hard to tell if the record is complete."

"The record is not complete, Sam, I can assure you of that."

"What do you mean?"

"It's what the Matriarchs have already figured out," Oscar

said. "The numbers don't add up. Money ... a lot of money ... has gone missing. Probably off the books. That explains why Laura and her crew are watching the DeSantis team like hawks. They want to know how much cash is hidden, and where it went."

"So all the paperwork isn't really what's important," Sam said. "We're trying to follow the money trail."

"Exactly, and that's why this is going to get dangerous. Care to join me for another martini before returning to the office?" Oscar asked.

In retrospect, Sam was glad he passed on the third drink. He would have been even more impaired, with an even slower reaction time, as they walked out of Billy's Grill.

Sam saw the old blue Buick just before it jumped the curb, aimed squarely at the two woozy lawyers. He pushed Oscar into a few other people on the sidewalk who were also in the heavy car's path.

Miraculously, no one got hurt as the blue Buick changed course and lurched back onto the street. The license plate was obscured, and its driver kept his head down as he sped away. Sam got a quick whiff of the Buick's exhaust, mixed with the smell of burning rubber. There were a few marks left on the sidewalk. No one even had time to scream.

Because this was Manhattan, where traffic near-misses happen all the time, the street almost immediately returned to normal. Perhaps the old blue Buick just suddenly lost control and jumped the curb outside the front entrance to Billy's Grill. Perhaps not. It happened so fast that the restaurant's doorman was just now coming down to make sure that one of his favorite patrons hadn't been hurt.

Oscar came through it without a wrinkle in his tailored silk suit. Sam ripped the sleeve on his more modest jacket as he scraped against the building.

"Are you all right?" Sam asked, grabbing the older man's arm to steady him.

Oscar checked himself over just to be sure before saying, "I'm fine, thanks." When he saw the rip on Sam's jacket, he added, "And, along with my gratitude, I owe you a new suit."

"I think the clothes are the least of our worries," Sam said, starting to feel his blood pressure return to normal. "That wasn't an accident, was it?"

"Well, given the current context, I'd say probably not," the senior counsel replied. "Now I know how Albert Rose felt."

Sixteen

Sam didn't anticipate the weekend ahead. He thought he was due for a break after the near-miss outside of Billy's Grill.

The Matriarchs actually had a name for their next tactic: "Standby Weekend Torture." Much different than almost being hit by a blue Buick. More drawn out, like many maneuvers at corporate law firms.

It started Friday night. Sam had worked all day on a summary memo for Robert, detailing a number of legal transactions at one of the DeSantis subsidiaries. For Sam, it was a distraction. He wanted to follow the money trail, with inside information provided by Oscar. That wasn't what the Matriarchs had in mind, and certainly did not fit with their method of breaking down yet another bright young lawyer in the service of Oscar Sampson.

Robert didn't acknowledge the initial summary memo until late Friday afternoon when Sam e-mailed a few revisions from one of the other DeSantis associates. "Too late, I've already sent it on to the next level for review," said Robert's text. "Quickly resend if anything is glaringly obvious."

"Nope, just little punctuation stuff," Sam wrote. The kind of stuff lawyers could spend a whole weekend parsing, as he was about to learn.

But the Matriarchs didn't want to ring the starting bell so

soon. They had all weekend to play out this script.

At 6p.m. on Friday, Sam looked over at Robert's office. The door was closed, and lights were out. A sure signal it was okay to go home, and that the summary memo was fine for its planned distribution on Monday. Sandi had left just a few minutes before, saying she had an old college friend in for the weekend. Sam hoped the old college friend was a girl, but didn't ask.

"Standby Weekend Torture" formally began at 07:53:19 Saturday morning (at least, that was the time stamp on the e-mail). Sam noticed the red light flashing on his Fish Fone as he stumbled out of bed around nine.

"I need someone to work on this for me *now* because I am getting on the phone," Robert wrote. "First, we need to make the minor corrections you said were needed yesterday. An additional correction is noted at the end of this e-mail trail." The new addition was a clarification of one of the financial projections in the document, no big deal. Sam couldn't tell the source of the correction, because Robert had removed it before forwarding the e-mail.

Sam decided to send a proactive e-mail before he'd even had coffee. Consistent with the image of the good team player he wanted to project, he wrote: "Good morning. Happy to process revisions as needed. Who else are we waiting to hear from, other than this initial correction?"

Robert wouldn't tell him. "Our colleagues are looking at the summary memo and will have more corrections," said his e-mail. "Send revision, and stand by."

Sam fired up his laptop, inserted the minor corrections and the financial clarification, sent it back to Robert as "Revision 2," and turned on the coffeemaker.

By the time Sam had his customary two cups of coffee, things started to get a little crazy. Robert forwarded someone's unsigned clarification to the original memo, which meant some on the weekend torture committee were looking at the first document, some the second. Robert had both versions floating out there.

Robert sent Sam a message saying, "these latest corrections are to the obsolete older version, yes?"

Sam instantly replied, "Yes, you now have two versions, with latest comments responding to the first one." And then, if only to take a stab at putting things back on track, Sam typed, "Who else is reviewing, and which version are they working off of?"

Robert didn't respond. Thinking he was probably working out the discrepancies, and there was actually a reason for the secrecy, Sam knew he had to stand by. For now, give Robert the benefit of the doubt. And watch cartoons. And eat breakfast. And get his gym gear together so that when this thing was done, he could work out.

About an hour later, Sam's Fish Fone started flashing. Robert was forwarding direction from someone (again, the source was cut off), indicating "strategic objectives" of the summary memo, which included "bolstering the DeSantis subsidiary's reputation for excellence, reassuring various government regulators of its stability and quality, reassuring its customers of its strong leadership, and not needlessly burdening its employees." *Adding Mom and apple pie to a financial summary*, Sam wondered?

Sam had enough coffee in him to respond like the lawyer he was, and typed: "This latest input suggests strategic objectives, but are not necessarily relevant additions to this document." It was correct, and worth a shot, but destined to fail.

Robert was quick with his response this time: "Please incorporate strategic objectives and earlier corrections into a new revision, which we can forward into a new document to short-circuit the now-competing revisions." Sam wondered why Robert wasn't just making all the minor revisions himself. By referring everything to Sam for cutting and pasting, he was essentially guaranteeing that whoever was editing would have competing and confusing versions. Likely part of the weekend plan.

Sam put everything he had together, and forwarded a new revision to Robert. This had now been going on a couple of hours, and Sam hoped to do other things this Saturday than "stand by."

The latest revision seemed to be satisfying the unnamed committee. No response from Robert to Revision #3. Sam made a sandwich, and put the Fish Fone on his desk so he'd see any flashing alert.

Another hour of standby passed. Nothing. Sam watched the trees outside his apartment windows, and responded to his personal e-mail. He even cleaned the bathroom, a little.

It was getting well into the afternoon, and Sam's gym closed at 6 p.m. on Saturdays. Sam changed out of the t-shirt and shorts he wore to sleep, and into the t-shirt and shorts he wore to the gym. He held the Fish Fone in his hand on the way to the gym, just in case.

He also carried the Fish Fone with him as he began his workout. About 15 minutes after his arrival at the gym, the familiar red light started to flash.

After hearing nothing from Robert for three hours, during which time Sam was apparently expected to stand by, Robert sent a text as if they had talked in the last five minutes: "We need to recharacterize the paragraph noted below to increase clarity and expand its scope," he typed. Sam realized that if he finished his workout, the soonest he'd be able to get home and create a revised document would be an hour from now. That could characterize him as not enough of a Fishbein team player. Sam didn't know much about being a double agent, but he figured that at minimum it meant working both sides.

So he tried to buy a little time, sending Robert a throw-away follow-up question while he went to the gym's locker room, grabbed his stuff, and jogged back home.

An hour later, the only sweat Sam had broken had been hustling back to his apartment. But he was quickly able to send Robert another revision, with the offending paragraph recast. He'd rewritten it in his head on the jog home.

Robert did respond this time. "Have sent on your revision. Hope everyone is now on the same page. Stand by."

Everyone was on the same page, Sam figured. *All the Matriarchs were on the page against Oscar Sampson and therefore me,* as the weekend turned into revision after revision after revision. Sam was tied to the Fish Fone Saturday afternoon, Saturday night, and all day Sunday. Eight reworkings of the same material. The summary document didn't really change much, certainly not enough to reflect the amount of Sam's weekend devoted to it.

The revised document wasn't the point. *The point was power,* Sam thought to himself. The Matriarchs wanted Sam to know that, whatever old tales Oscar Sampson was planting in his head, their control of Fishbein was almost complete.

It left Sam with just one question. Robert had been with Fishbein, Schindler, Rose and Sampson for about five years. He'd obviously spent most of that time "standing by" himself for the Matriarchs. Sam wondered at what point and for what reasons Robert allowed himself to be reduced to the Matriarch's errand boy. Was it money, or was it fear?

Sam understood the money part, since he too was cashing the Matriarchs' checks. But, Sam wondered, *what was Robert afraid of?*

Seventeen

Sandi caved to the Matriarchs on the subject of professional dress. If they wanted her to be drab and sexless, she could do drab and sexless. Sandi certainly didn't want to become the object of the Matriarchs' wrath. They were in charge, and everyone knew it.

Sandi was at her cubicle, wearing a new light blue business suit that was not her but was definitely them. White blouse underneath, indicating no hint of cleavage, and sensible heels. Sam noticed, but didn't say anything. He thought Sandi's decision to fit in and lay low was smart, under the circumstances.

But letting Sandi stay below the radar was not what the Matriarchs had in mind. Connie, Fishbein's Director of Legal Recruiting, was on the phone, asking Sandi if she had time for lunch. "Of course, I'd love to join you," Sandi said, understanding that no one turned down an invitation to lunch with the Matriarchs.

Sandi thought she might end up in the Fishbein cafeteria, at a corner table eating a subsidized salad. Instead, Matriarch Connie invited Sandi to the Client Conference Floor.

It was quite possible to get lost on Fishbein's Client Conference Floor. It was a gilded maze. The whole idea was to impress prospective new clients, and intimidate anyone else called to a meeting with Fishbein lawyers. The carpets were plush, the woodwork was mahogany, and modern photography graced the walls, including some of the best pictures ever taken of New York City's 9-11 "Twin Towers of Light" memorial in 2002. "Fishbein, Schindler, Rose and Sampson" appeared very discreetly on the front of the reception desk, in a shiny metal script that could've been silver or platinum.

The catering staff on the Client Conference Floor put out a beautiful buffet every day, open from 12 noon until 2 p.m. Fishbein lawyers and clients could pick up a plate, fill it with that day's seafood or steak selection, and get right back to their meetings within the Floor's maze of conference rooms. Luxurious, yet efficient service for a firm billing premium New York rates. Everyone ate well, but no time was wasted with restaurants and waiters.

Connie met Sandi in the Floor's reception area with a brisk, "Hi, great to see you! There's seafood on the buffet today!"

The Matriarch and her new recruit put the minimum necessary calories on their plates, and then went to the small conference room Connie had reserved for the occasion. Two more Matriarchs, Carol and Mindy, were already seated inside. Nodding and smiling, they seemed pleased that their sartorial criticisms at the previous staff meeting had registered with Sandi, and that she had redone her wardrobe to their specifications.

"Sandi, we've all been wondering how things have been going for you, now that you've had a little time under your belt," said Connie, who had actively recruited Sandi from law school. "We thought it was time for a girls' lunch."

"I appreciate the opportunity to get together with you," Sandi said. She may have come from a second-tier school, but Sandi knew a job interview when she saw one, and had been trained to perform.

"Has everyone been providing you a proper welcome?" asked Carol, the Matriarch in charge of the firm's finances, who was already fiddling with her designer eyeglasses. Carol didn't have much patience for pleasantries.

"Everything has been just fine," Sandi said, already wondering what the Matriarchs really had in mind for the lunch menu. She was hoping it didn't include young female associates, served rare and vulnerable. "Fishbein has a reputation as being the best in the business, and I'm beginning to understand why."

"We're very proud of what we've built here, and see nothing but smooth sailing ahead," Carol said, sounding very much like a CFO just off a conference call with investment analysts.

Sandi was the investment under consideration today. The first step was to impress her with the firm's feminist-friendly history.

"We've tried to make Fishbein a place where ambitious women would feel welcome, and find the flexibility to pursue their career goals," Connie said. "As you remember from our recruiting interviews, we're consistently ranked in the first tier by women's legal organizations."

"It's a reputation borne out by facts and history," Sandi said, shifting almost effortlessly into law-student-at-an-interview mode. So far, this was easier than trying to adjust to the Matriarch's fashion sense.

"Laura's not with us today, but her ears would burn to hear this praise," Carol said. "So much of what we've been able to accomplish is because of the trail she cleared for us decades ago. It's really because of her that we've come so far."

"I understand she was at the side of Mr. Fishbein almost from the beginning," Sandi said.

"That's true, and keep in mind she didn't have your excellent legal training," Carol said. Sandi wasn't used to hearing her Fordham legal education described as "excellent," especially in comparison to Ivy Leaguers like Sam. She liked it.

"Morris Fishbein built this firm by taking the work the 'white shoe' firms didn't want to do, like bankruptcies," Carol continued, knowing she was describing the specialty Sandi was now concentrating on, much to the firm's profit. "He hired the right people, women like Laura Henderson. And Laura saw what Morris Fishbein could not see."

"What could Mr. Fishbein not see?" Sandi asked, genuinely interested.

"That his repudiation of the established law firms needed a complement on the business side."

Connie jumped in: "To be blunt, Sandi, and to acknowledge that this isn't a matter we discuss during initial interviews with law students, Morris Fishbein was ahead of the curve on generating law firm business. But not in the actual operation of a law firm."

Sandi looked perplexed.

"The old boy network was starting to die," Carol said. "Morris Fishbein built a law firm on the business the old boys didn't want."

"And then kept it growing by developing techniques the old boys wouldn't use," Connie added. "Hostile takeovers. Poison pills. Morris took the floor right out from under them, and found kindred souls in Schindler and Rose."

Sandi noticed the omission of the one still-living partner, Oscar Sampson. The purpose of this friendly lunch meeting was starting to come into focus.

"Corporate law is a tough business, Sandi," said Mindy, the Director of Case Management, who decided it was time to put down her fork. "We are very successful women, operating a global business, and we have every intention of staying on top."

"I'm here to help," Sandi said. "Is there something in particular you need from me?"

"As a matter of fact, there is," Mindy continued. "You know the DeSantis restructuring as well as anyone on the team. How is it going so far?"

"I'm sure you've read the summary reports," Sandi said. "It's complicated. There are a lot of players, a lot of history, and a lot of connections we're still trying to figure out. The money part is a mess."

"We know all that," Mindy said. "Listen, Sandi, let me cut to the chase. DeSantis is very important to us. We don't trust all the information we've been getting, and there is no way to deny that one of our named partners may not have the firm's best interests at heart."

"I understand," Sandi said, though she didn't understand the Matriarchs at all. "What can I do?"

"We want to be able to trust you as an extra set of eyes and ears for us," Connie said, adopting the tone she had used so successfully with Sandi during their early job interviews.

"And we want you to keep an eye on the guy in the next cubicle, Sam Mitcham."

Eighteen

Sam was in his cubicle, just back from grabbing a sandwich at the Fishbein cafeteria, waiting for Sandi to return from her lunch with the Matriarchs. She hadn't been targeted by a blue Buick, Sam thought, but had been made to feel complicit in the firings of two secretaries, and had to deal with a literal and humiliating dressing-down at the last staff meeting. Sam thought perhaps the Matriarchs had an easier time intimidating and recruiting young women to their cause than young men, but then he remembered what a tool they had made of poor Robert.

Sam's personal cell phone on his cubicle desk started flashing, and the caller ID indicated his Mom was on the line. He picked it up immediately, knowing Barbara Mitcham wouldn't be calling her son during business hours unless she had to.

"Hey Mom, what's up?"

"I'm at the hospital. Theresa and I just had a meeting with the oncologist. The news isn't good."

"Tell me."

"All the chemo and radiation aren't working. Theresa's leukemia is not going into remission. The oncologist thinks they need to do something else."

"Like what?"

"Like a bone marrow transplant."

Sam sighed. He had read all the literature, and he knew bone marrow transplants had become a much more common procedure, with an always-improving chance of success. Still, whenever anyone is confronted with the realistic option of a bone marrow transplant, they sigh.

Barbara Mitcham soldiered on, knowing she had Sam's full attention. "As her biological sibling, you have the best chance of being able to donate bone marrow for her."

"Okay, so what do I do?" Sam asked.

"The oncologist says there are a number of places in New York where you can get tested."

"Or I could come there."

"Yeah, or you could come here."

"Let me see what our friend Oscar can do. I'll get right back to you." Sam ended the call, and raced up to Oscar Sampson's office. This time, he didn't care if Robert was watching his path.

Oscar was expecting him. Sam had evidently been Barbara Mitcham's second call.

"I'm sorry to hear about Theresa," Oscar said, and looked as though he meant it. "Another tough break."

"I know," Sam said.

"Turns out we need to go back to DeSantis headquarters in Chicago. Taking off this afternoon work for you? I'll have Robert make the arrangements."

"My apartment is five blocks away. I'll go home and pack."

The airlines have flights between New York and Chicago every hour, like a shuttle. When money was no object, lawyers could move from the East Coast to the Midwest very quickly. Oscar went from O'Hare airport to his usual Chicago hotel. Sam went from O'Hare to Milwaukee. He kept the Fish Fone on the rental car seat, just to keep up necessary appearances at Fishbein, Schindler, Rose and Sampson.

Sam had been talking to his sister almost every day on the

phone. He noticed her voice was growing faint, but he attributed that to all the chemotherapy. Sam wasn't prepared for what faced him inside her room on the cancer floor. His mother tried to warn him about his sister's deterioration.

Theresa looked even more like an old man than before, and a very sick old man at that. Sunken eyes, pale skin, bald, wearing one of those ridiculous open-at-the-back hospital gowns, hooked up to blinking machines. Sam swallowed hard a couple of times before he could say anything. He was grateful for the required surgical mask, intended to prevent further infection, but also preventing the patient from seeing the expression of horror on the faces of visitors.

Theresa had been dealing with cancer for a couple of years now. First breast cancer, then the secondary leukemia. To the extent it's possible, she was used to feeling like hell. And now it was worse. The treatment wasn't working.

"Turns out this leukemia is at least as stubborn as members of the Mitcham family," Theresa said, by way of greeting.

"Yeah," Sam sighed again. "I was hoping we'd have you out of here by now."

Theresa and Sam's Mom was there to state the obvious: "Not much has been happening according to our plans lately. But we always have options."

The oncologist joined them, knowing Sam would want to hear the options. Reading online reports and hematology journal articles was one thing, but right now everyone wanted to hear from an oncologist with practical knowledge and experience.

"As you know, we've had some success with the current treatment of chemotherapy and radiation, but don't think we're going to be able to get the leukemia into remission and keep it there," she said. "Unfortunately, Theresa has a very difficult form of the disease."

No one said anything. The Mitcham family trusted their oncologist, and just wanted to be told what to do. Sam wondered how many of these difficult conversations the oncologist had to initiate every day. It gave him a little additional perspective on his relative degree of difficulty being a corporate lawyer. Of course, Sam's double agent situation was unique, but none of that mattered right now in this hospital room.

"A bone marrow transplant offers the opportunity to begin anew," said the oncologist. "Here's how it works: Once we find the best possible match, we use even more chemo to take Theresa's immune system down to zero. We infuse her with the bone marrow transplant, and encourage it to take up residence in its new host. Theresa gets a new immune system, and we closely monitor her to minimize the possibility of any recurrence of the leukemia or other complications."

Bottom line, thought Sam: *my sister is a very sick lady. But maybe I can help. It certainly makes more sense than whatever I've gotten into at the Big Fish.*

"Sam, we know your time is limited," said the oncologist.

Sam couldn't help the few tears that started to leave dark spots on his surgical mask. His mother's mask looked the same.

"Okay, let's go," was all Sam could say.

He was whisked off to another room for the Bone Marrow Transplant Team to do its testing. They did cheek swabs and took blood. Given what his sister was enduring in the other room, Sam wished he could do more. The idea of being her bone marrow donor, even if it meant enduring a painful procedure including a thick extraction needle shot into his lower back, would be welcomed in a heartbeat.

But Sam Mitcham, Theresa Mitcham, and Barbara Mitcham were not getting their prayers answered these days.

Sam's bone marrow was not a match with his sister's.

Nineteen

Sometimes getting back to work is a relief. This was one of those times. Sam knew that while he was racing to DeSantis Industries in Chicago, the Milwaukee crew would try to find a donor for his sister.

Oscar Sampson and Peter DeSantis tried to offer comfort in their time-tested venue – lunch at Chicago's Mercantile Club. They were seated immediately upon arrival at their usual table.

Peter DeSantis knew a lot about business, but like most people, didn't know anything about bone marrow transplants.

"So, why wouldn't you be a match for your sister?" he asked.

"It's all chemistry and biology," Sam said. "There are certain chemical markers they look for. First, you have to pass a minimum threshold of markers to be considered a potential match at all. Once you pass the threshold, the more markers you have in common, the better the match. You could have a couple of potential matches among siblings in a single family. One might be better than the others, just based on how many markers above the threshold each person has."

"And where did you land?"

"I didn't land at all. I didn't pass the minimum threshold. My bone marrow would kill her."

"Sort of like blood types," DeSantis said. "Sometimes they attract, sometimes they repel?"

"Yeah, like blood types … but a lot more complicated. Sometimes a match isn't perfect, but if it's all they've got, they go for it."

"So, what happens now?" DeSantis asked.

"A lot of people around the country have been tested, and are listed in a national directory. They're going through the directory right now."

"Does that usually work?" Peter DeSantis was a corporate executive who liked to ask questions. It's how he figured things out.

"We'll find out, and hopefully soon. Theresa's immune system can't fight both the leukemia and the treatment for the leukemia, at least not indefinitely."

Peter DeSantis allowed himself one moment of pure bombast, directed at his friend and business partner Oscar Sampson: "Oscar, maybe we should've put our heads together on this one, rather than building a transportation network. Bet we could've figured it out."

Oscar cut him off. "How about your mother, kid? Could she be a match?"

"Women typically aren't very good candidates for bone marrow donors after they've had children. Some of the components of their blood, specifically their antigen levels, change in the process."

"You've been on the receiving end of mountains of legal filings, audit records, and merger notes. Where did you find the time to learn so much about this?" Oscar said, sincerely impressed with the information processing abilities of Barbara Mitcham's son.

"You find time for family," Sam said.

The Mercantile Club's ancient waiters responded to the silence at the table by refilling everyone's drink.

Finally Peter DeSantis spoke. "We're rooting for you and your family, kid."

"I appreciate that," Sam said. "It's going to take some time before we know what's what. Not an unfamiliar feeling." It was an attempt to lighten up the mood at the table, complemented by a warm smile from Sam, and it worked.

"Well, to the business at hand, I don't think the web at DeSantis Industries is as tangled as some are making it out to be," said DeSantis. "This is not a dime store we've been running."

"No, sir, everyone gets that."

"And I know those women back in New York you have to contend with … and Oscar has to contend with … aren't making things any easier for anyone."

"If I can be blunt, sir, this is my first major restructuring. I don't have earlier experience to compare it to."

"Well, let me tell you what's getting lost in all this, if I may," Peter DeSantis said, looking at Oscar as much for permission as he was to Sam. Both senior and junior lawyer nodded.

"The idea of tearing down what we've built up breaks my heart. Maybe I didn't dot every i and cross every t, but no one does – especially when they've fought the battles I had to fight every day here in Chicago."

"I've read that the Addison Trucking merger was a real ball-breaker," Sam said. His language was a little saltier than he'd normally employ at a business lunch, but the Mercantile Club waiters had kept the martinis flowing.

"I didn't mean the difficulty growing the business," DeSantis said. "And I didn't mean the deals we cut. I could defend each and every piece of it."

Sam simply nodded. Peter DeSantis clearly wanted Sam to listen, not talk.

"I know that lawyers have been poring over the executive compensation reports. Those are always juicy targets at a time like this. And, in the same way I could defend each and every deal we made, I can also defend what we paid our employees, what we paid our executives, what we paid our counsel, and what I took home myself."

Sam kept nodding. Oscar sipped his martini.

"Let me tell you something else. I know this is old-school of me, but I never forgot the best businesses not only take from their communities, they give back to them. You won't find this in any of the securities filings, but guess who is a patron of 63 … count 'em, 63 charities in the Chicago area?"

"I knew the DeSantis name was connected to significant philanthropic efforts, but didn't know the details," said Sam.

"Well, no one else seems to care now that the knives are out, but I'm here to tell you a few," said the still-president and CEO of DeSantis Industries. "Hospitals. Clinics. Universities. Museums. You think Chicago theatre would be in the same league as New York without me?"

Sam knew a rant when he heard one, but he had to respect a guy as sure of himself as Peter DeSantis.

"With your constant help, Oscar, I've built a business I'm proud of. It's been my life's work. And now, because of those shrill women back in New York, I'm getting run out of town. Does that strike you as fair, kid?"

"It certainly doesn't, sir," Sam said, wondering if Oscar had told Peter that he was here to help. Double agent and everything.

"And what about you, Oscar?" DeSantis decided to aim, below the belt, at his friend of decades. "Last time I looked at one of your hefty invoices, wasn't your name still on the letterhead? Why is this happening?"

Oscar Sampson shifted in his chair a little, but said nothing.

Sam wondered if there was a way to steer the conversation back to his family troubles. He preferred Peter DeSantis' sympathy to his rising anger, however misdirected it was at the named founding partner and first year associate of Fishbein, Schindler, Rose and Sampson.

Twenty

"Restructuring" is a nicer word than "bankruptcy," Peter DeSantis thought on the drive home from his office. Oscar Sampson had talked him through it a hundred times. The legal texts define it as a reorganization of the legal, financial, and operational structures of a company to make it more profitable, or to fix specific problems. Nasty baggage like past-due bills to creditors are renegotiated or swept away. Stockholders can lose their entire investment.

It just isn't fair, DeSantis thought, looking past Lake Shore Drive onto the open expanse of Lake Michigan. All the work he had done for the soul of his hometown, and all the largesse he had showered upon its cultural and service sectors, didn't matter much right now. The bottom line was that the company had taken on too much debt, interest rates and loan terms had changed in ways that no one saw coming, and now the bills were coming due.

It was getting complicated, not just because of the size of DeSantis Industries, with all those divisions and their employees, but because no one really knew where all the money was. So the Fishbein lawyers and internal accountants were trying to find it. DeSantis had cut a lot of deals in the past few decades, ably assisted by Oscar Sampson on most of them. There was a lot to go through.

This isn't working out the way I planned, thought DeSantis, glancing for just a moment at the speedometer. Twenty miles per hour over the limit. DeSantis didn't care. He had friends at the Police Department.

I covered every possible base, he thought. As DeSantis Industries grew, Peter DeSantis became a regular on the Chicago business circuit. He dined at the Mercantile Club. He joined the Business Roundtable. He accepted invitations to serve on boards of directors. He wanted to be of service, and wanted to connect with business leaders as emboldened by ambition, vision and foresight as he had been.

Peter DeSantis had a beautiful penthouse apartment near the top of Chicago's John Hancock Center, served by a private elevator. He steered his midnight blue Jaguar into the basement parking garage right off of Michigan Avenue, pulled onto his private parking deck, walked through the sliding door into the elevator, and was whisked upstairs.

Bernice was dusting his desk as he got off the penthouse elevator. "Hello, sir," his housekeeper said, then briskly added, "I sorted all of today's mail into piles."

DeSantis could see the stacks sitting on his giant desk. One of the piles was at least twice as tall as the others, plumped up by the thick and expensively-printed invitations to the fundraising galas of Chicago's cultural institutions. Peter DeSantis was on every VIP list, and many of the invitations featured fine calligraphy, expressing hope that he could attend. And contribute.

"Once they have your name, you never go off the list," Bernice said, smiling at her longtime employer. "I'm done here, unless you need anything else."

"I'm fine. Thank you, everything is top-notch, as always," said DeSantis. "Have a nice evening," he said, as Bernice left the room and exited the penthouse via the front door.

With the pending restructuring, which was not yet known even by the business press, Peter DeSantis worked hard to keep up appearances. Anything less could adversely affect the value of his stock, and the retirement portfolios of his employees.

It was so much extra work, he thought, *keeping up appearances*. He started leafing through the thick invitations. The Art Institute of Chicago's exhibition opening. Another premier at the Goodman Theatre. Something from the Lifesource Blood Center Corporate Volunteer Leadership Board. DeSantis always replied "yes" to these offers of civic involvement, with a check included in his RSVP.

The strain had started to show, though. Even with the morning workouts at his home gym, he put on more pounds than he wanted. Of course, Peter DeSantis was never one to turn down the offer of a fine meal or drink, and he did not count calories. The doctors had said his blood pressure, cholesterol and triglycerides were all fine for a man of his age and condition. If he had problems, they were luxury problems.

After the news of the untimely death of Oscar Sampson's partner Albert Rose, DeSantis briefly wondered whether he should consider a bodyguard. He dismissed the idea, rationalizing that Albert Rose's death may have been questionable, but Rose never had much to do with the Chicago business. Oscar Sampson was his man, and his trusted friend. The many Fishbein associates who did the grunt work stayed for a couple of years, then left. The ones who wanted to go to Chicago sometimes ended up at DeSantis Industries as in-house counsel.

Oscar was a good judge of talent, and a good trainer of baby lawyers, DeSantis thought, as he poured a glass of fine scotch from the bar. Sam Mitcham looked to be his brightest yet, and with the boy's ties to the Midwest, he might become important to a restructured DeSantis Industries ... or whatever it was called after it emerged from Bankruptcy Court.

Peter DeSantis had held out some hope that he could pull a rabbit out of his hat, and stop this whole restructuring process in its tracks. Oscar Sampson was on the lookout for rabbits as well. The odds were seriously against them, and they knew it.

Reflecting his own concern at Albert Rose's death, Oscar

had once wondered aloud about bodyguards for both of them. DeSantis counseled his friend and lawyer against it. "For all you know, your so-called Matriarchs had nothing to do with the death of Albert Rose," he'd said. "Do you want to live in fear of a bunch of bitches?"

At the time, Oscar and Peter toasted to living their lives as they always had – confident, fearless, and counting on continued success. Experience was the best indicator of the future, they agreed, and there was no reason to alter their fantastically successful formula. They were both millionaires many times over, and still having fun at their jobs. Especially when they were both in Chicago, and Oscar was away from the Matriarchs.

If Sam had been privy to everything going on, and the details of all the deals Peter DeSantis and Oscar Sampson had cut, he would've urged caution. Bodyguards, or enhanced security of some sort, might have been a good idea.

Peter DeSantis was, for all his history in a notoriously bottom-line city like Chicago, a smart businessman with a big heart. He took care of his people, partly because that was the way he was built, but also because he knew it was good business. He had the Hancock Center penthouse apartment, the midnight blue Jaguar parked on the private deck, Bernice the housekeeper, stocks, cash, and happy employees to prove it.

Peter DeSantis had made a lot of friends in the health-care arena. He knew that whatever Sam and his family were doing to find a donor for Theresa, he could do one better. Behind the large desk in his penthouse office, he started making calls, with a target list including the heads of foundations, the CEOs of medical centers, and the leaders of the Midwest's biggest HMOs. If Peter DeSantis was on the phone, asking them to make sure that a woman named Theresa Mitcham got every possible consideration in the national search for a bone marrow match, she would go from wherever she was to the top of the list. If Sam had known that DeSantis was trying to help, he would've been grateful.

But Peter DeSantis never got very far down his call list. The phone records from his Hancock Center penthouse would record outgoing calls to the home phone numbers of the CEOs at the National Marrow Donor Program and the University of Chicago School of Medicine. The last call went out at 9:04p.m.

By 9:06p.m., Peter DeSantis was dead.

J.D. FOX

Twenty-One

Sam was at his Chicago four-star Fishbein-approved hotel, on his cell phone returning a call from Sandi. She'd expressed concern about Theresa's condition, and he was bringing her up to speed on the intricacies of the bone marrow donation process. And his frustration at not being an acceptable donor himself. By chance, he also had the television tuned to one of the local Chicago stations, which was now in the initial headlines of its early evening newscast.

The death of Peter DeSantis was the lead story on "Eyewitness News at Five," and Sam immediately recognized the picture over the news anchor's shoulder, with a banner "Mogul Murder?" splashed across it.

"Hey, there's a story on TV right now saying Peter DeSantis is dead." Sam's eyes were wide with disbelief.

"Huh? You were just with him," Sandi said.

"I know, hang on." Sam grabbed the remote, and turned up the volume on the television. Details were few, but the conclusion seemed certain. Peter DeSantis had been shot to death at his home.

"This is unbelievable," Sandi muttered, and grabbed her laptop to check the story online. It was everywhere, as a bulletin from the Associated Press, already asking whether the professional-looking hit was mob-related.

Then Sam's Fish Fone started flashing. Robert was forwarding the AP bulletin. And, asking where Oscar Sampson was.

Chicago media are as competitive as in any big city, maybe more so. And "spot news" like a celebrity murder automatically trumped anything else, especially for ratings-conscious local TV stations. Sam turned up the volume on his room's television so Sandi could hear the live reports.

"Dave, the first thing we heard, from our sources at the Police Department, was the initial call of a homicide at the John Hancock Center," said reporter Jim Simmons at the scene. Eyewitness News at Five knew that someone killed at a good address is always a bigger story than someone killed at a bad address.

Sam tried to describe what Sandi could hear but not see on the Chicago news station. "There are cops, flashing red lights, and television cameras all over the place," he said.

Jim Simmons continued his live report, saying, "Dave, the next thing we heard, again from our police sources, was that a body had been discovered on the top residential floor. Everyone knows the top floor is where Peter DeSantis lived, and sometimes lavishly entertained."

"Jim, doesn't his home occupy the *entire* top floor?" asked Dave Daniels, the Eyewitness News anchorman. "We understand he's a millionaire many times over, if not a billionaire."

Behind the live picture of Jim Simmons talking into an Eyewitness News microphone, Sam could see police running bright yellow "Crime Scene – Do Not Enter" tape around the perimeter of the building. Guards were being posted every 20 feet, and Jim Simmons said all residents were now being checked for identification before being allowed inside.

"Peter DeSantis isn't the only famous resident of the John Hancock Center," said Dave Daniels.

"He certainly isn't, Dave," said Jim Simmons. The other famous residents included a national talk-show host and a few hedge fund billionaires. They decided to wait out the next day or two at their other residences. The servants could keep an eye on the cats and plants.

City cops were swarming the place by the time the medical examiner arrived. The coroner in such cases didn't share the urgency of Dave Daniels, Jim Simmons, and the growing crowd outside. After all, it was a reasonable certainty that the subject of all this fuss was indeed dead.

"What else can you tell us, Jim?" asked Dave Daniels. "It looks like chaos behind you."

"Dave, we understand that a body, perhaps the body of Peter DeSantis, was found slumped in his chair," said the reporter. "I understand that he had a list of names in front of him. He may have been making some phone calls."

"Any signs of a struggle?" asked Dave Daniels.

"We haven't heard those details yet," said Jim Simmons. "We'll of course let you know immediately if we do."

"Do the police have any witnesses?" was the next question from Dave Daniels in the studio.

"We don't think so," said the reporter. "Police sources, off the record, indicate that the victim was shot to death, with an unconfirmed report of two bullet wounds to the head. Apparently no one heard the shots."

"So, perhaps a silencer was used," said Dave Daniels, trying to squeeze as much news as he could from the crime scene. "On the other hand, with a whole floor in a concrete and steel skyscraper, one wouldn't expect noise to bother the neighbors."

"There's a lot of speculation right now," said Jim Simmons. "All we know for sure is that Chicago Police are investigating a homicide involving a firearm. The victim may be Peter DeSantis, but we don't have official confirmation of that yet."

"Jim, we have a comment from police," said Dave Daniels. "Let's roll that videotape."

The police officer thrown in front of the hungry television

cameras looked terrified, and befuddled. "All we're able to say right now, pending notification of kin, is that we are investigating a possible homicide," he said, over and over, answering every question with the only thing he was authorized to say.

Inside the Hancock Center crime scene, for Chicago's detectives, there wasn't much to work with. No signs of forced entry. No one saw anything. The lobby's security videotapes looked clear, for what that was worth. Peter DeSantis had a private elevator from the parking garage to his penthouse apartment, with no security camera recording visitors entering or leaving his private sanctuary. His body had been discovered by his longtime housekeeper Bernice on her late afternoon rounds, so it was quite possible that some time had passed since the fatal shooting.

So little information, so many questions. The television station continued its live reporting, Sam kept watching, and Sandi listened on her cell phone.

"Who else lived in the Hancock Center?" asked Dave Daniels. "Why would anyone target rich people like the residents there? Could there be other victims? Was this the work of professionals, or a crime of passion?"

Jim Simmons restated everything he knew, which didn't include anything new. It didn't matter. People were tuning in as word spread, and the story was updated whenever a reporter was able to get some new tidbit from their police sources. In the absence of anything new, they would repeat what they had.

"Don't you think you should check in with Oscar?" Sandi asked Sam. "Where is he?"

"He's probably in his room, but I don't know for sure," Sam said. "Robert was asking about him too."

"Call him on the hotel phone," Sandi instructed.

Keeping Sandi on the cell phone, and the television on, Sam picked up the land line in his room, and asked the hotel operator to connect him to Mr. Sampson.

The phone rang a few times before Oscar picked it up. "Yes?" he said formally.

"It's Sam. Have you heard about Peter DeSantis?"

"I'm afraid I have. What terrible news. What have you heard?"

Sam told Oscar what he remembered of the bulletin and television story.

"My God, my dear friend, dead."

"I'm so sorry."

"Thank you," said Oscar, realizing that he had obligations as counsel that would require his immediate attention. "I'm going to make a few calls, and I'll call you back. Please stay near the phone."

"Absolutely, and one more thing. New York already knows about it. Robert sent me the Associated Press bulletin as I was watching the news. He wants to know where you are."

"Vultures. Okay, I'll call you right back."

Sam put down the land line, and picked up his cell phone. Sandi was still on it, and had heard the conversation with Oscar.

"This is unbelievable," she offered.

"Believe it, and since you're online, take another look at the news for me," he ordered.

"What am I looking for?"

"I don't mean to sound cold, but see if there's anything in the news other than typical crime reporting. Is there anything about the restructuring of DeSantis Industries?"

"That's really smart, Sam," Sandi said. "Definitely cold, but smart. I'm looking."

While she looked, Sam booted up his own laptop, and searched the financial news websites.

They both came to the same conclusion. Nothing, so far.

Then Sam's hotel phone rang. It was Oscar.

"Sam, we'll need to work tonight on a statement," he said, sounding several degrees colder than the lawyer-in-a-crisis mask Sam had just put on for Sandi. "It will come from the executive management of DeSantis Industries. It will note that they are shocked and appalled at the news of Peter DeSantis' death. It will further say that pending a full investigation and the search for those responsible for this heinous crime, business will continue. Because that is what Peter DeSantis would have wanted. Got it?"

"You bet. I'll go down to the hotel's business center. They have a printer there."

"No, get the concierge to set up a secure computer and printer in my suite. Number 1012. We'll work on the statement together."

Sam put down the land line, and picked up his cell phone.

"I think you're in for a long night," Sandi said.

"I was thinking the same thing."

"Go, do what you have to do," Sandi said. "Call if you need help with anything."

"Thank you," Sam said, as he put down his cell phone, turned off the television, ran out the door, down the stairs, and directly to the front desk. Tonight, this four-star hotel would earn its reputation for 24-hour service.

Twenty-Two

The assassination of a mogul was big news in Chicago, but it reverberated in New York, too. Especially since the mogul's law firm was based there.

The Matriarchs and Oscar Sampson didn't see eye-to-eye on much anymore, but this was about the survival of the firm. There was no difference in opinion on the topic of maintaining appearances in Chicago. It was appropriate for the partner in charge of the Chicago business to notify the firm's Chief Operating Officer.

"Laura, I'm calling to bring you up to date on our activities in Chicago," Oscar said.

"Oscar, I'm so sorry about this tragic turn of events," she began. "I know Peter DeSantis was your friend as well as your client."

"Thank you," he said. "I've reviewed the entire situation with our public relations firm."

"What is their counsel?" she asked.

"Peter's identity has already been confirmed," Oscar began. "I agreed that transparency would be our best policy."

"That sounds sensible," Laura said.

"Of course, the PR firm is now working to influence the news coverage," Oscar continued.

"How can that be done?" Laura asked.

"A list of the 63 Chicago charities supported by DeSantis Industries was distributed," Oscar said. "CEOs, foundation executives, and medical center presidents were made available to fill the media's requests for interviews, and to recall the vital importance of Peter DeSantis to Chicago."

"I completely concur with that strategy," Laura said. "What about the rumors about the financial health of DeSantis Industries?"

"Some leakage is unavoidable," Oscar said. "As you know, there are rumors that DeSantis has a mountain of bad debt, and would go bankrupt if its stock tanked."

"Those are very vivid images," Laura said. "And we both know they're more than rumors." She was on the speaker phone in her office, and suddenly began to stare at the symbol of her power as the First Matriarch, her pale blue diamond ring.

"Yes," he said, continuing to press. "And, on top of all the rumors surrounding the death of Albert Rose, this could be a very difficult time for the firm."

Laura paused for a moment. She wasn't expecting a reference to Albert Rose. She and Oscar had been maintaining silence on that.

"Specific to the DeSantis rumors in Chicago," Laura said, "how can we best address them?"

"Since it's just one day since Peter DeSantis was found dead, it's feasible to dismiss the Chicago rumors as mere speculation," Oscar said.

"It is in everyone's best interest to do so," Laura said.

"We'll likely get a much more conclusive coroner's report in Chicago than we did in New York for Albert Rose," Oscar said. "Peter DeSantis was shot at close range."

"Yes, that would be a significant difference between the deaths of Peter DeSantis and Albert Rose," Laura said. "One of many."

"I suppose so," he said. "And then there's the matter of my near-miss on the streets of New York City."

"Excuse me?" Laura asked.

"Luckily, other than an associate's torn jacket, no one was worse for the wear."

"Oscar, I don't know what you're referring to."

"Then there's nothing else to discuss." Oscar decided the conversation was over, for now. "I'm going to manage the situation in Chicago, and I'll keep Sam Mitcham with me," he said. "You and your team can continue the restructuring preparation, discreetly, back in New York."

For an individual telephone call, it was a bravura performance. After years as a corporate attorney, Oscar had learned to put aside personal emotion when needed. This was one of those times. He needed to prevent an immediate implosion at DeSantis Industries. He needed to be seen as a calming, fatherly presence. He needed to be there for the shocked employees who liked and respected Peter DeSantis. But he also wanted to send a signal to Laura Henderson.

"All right," Laura said. "What's next?"

"I need to do a few calming interviews for our media friends in Chicago," he replied.

"Is there anything more I need to do from here?"

"No, thanks," Oscar concluded. "You've done more than enough. I'll be back in touch should there be significant news."

Oscar took some small measure of satisfaction at handling Laura, at least for now. His next task would be easier.

Oscar Sampson had dealt with nosy reporters before, and knew how to be gracious while saying nothing. He instructed the PR firm to put him on the phone with reporters who would not accept the canned statement he and Sam had drafted. He could certainly swat down any rude suggestions of Chicago mob involvement or financial trouble at DeSantis Industries.

"Mr. Sampson, so sorry at the loss of your client and friend," said Danielle Larsen, a blonde news presenter from the Chicago Fox-TV affiliate. This was typical of the interviews Oscar would conduct in the DeSantis boardroom. Employees watched from the open doorway.

"Thank you. Everyone here is just devastated by the news. We've lost a good man, and a good friend."

"You were also Peter DeSantis' lawyer, isn't that right?"

"Well," Oscar slightly shrugged. "Peter DeSantis built a large, well-respected business here in Chicago. I'm just one of the lawyers who helped along the way."

Danielle Larsen probably wasn't aware that she was being handled by an expert. Danielle was mostly aware that she was having a bad hair day, and kept fussing with her bangs while asking additional questions. She was wearing the kind of outfit that definitely would have been banned by the Matriarchs – a very clingy sweater set with matching knee-high boots. Someone back at the station probably handed her a card with four questions written on it.

"The police don't have much to say about the murder. What can you tell us?"

"I'm confident Chicago's finest will bring the person or persons responsible for this crime to justice. In the meantime, everyone here is just starting to deal with the reality that Peter DeSantis is gone."

"Any truth to the rumors that this corporation was in financial trouble, or connected to organized crime?" Danielle asked.

Oscar had to be careful with this one on camera. Television statements have a nasty habit of coming back to bite you when they're contradicted later. So Oscar politely ignored the question. "Let me just say that DeSantis Industries is open for business. We understand our significant role in Chicago's economy, not to mention providing thousands of people with jobs, including yours truly." He nodded sincerely.

Danielle Larsen wrapped it up with a softball. "What do you

think the legacy of Peter DeSantis will be?"

"I think he'd want to be remembered as a man who had both brains and heart," Oscar said. "He built one of Chicago's leading businesses. At the same time, he gave back. He understood his important role in our community…not just providing jobs, but supporting the things people really care about. Schools. Hospitals. The Widows' and Orphans' Funds at the Police and Fire Departments. Everything that makes Chicago the great city it is. We've lost one of our best."

Oscar delivered similar remarks at the funeral of Peter DeSantis. Employees were given the day off. The downtown Chicago church was filled to overflowing. Many of the people who worked for Peter DeSantis wanted to pay their respects.

Sam had known Peter DeSantis for just a short time, but liked him. He was fun to be around, and he wore his power well. It seemed to suit him.

Sam was also aware that Peter DeSantis had been under considerable pressure to maintain a calm exterior while his business empire was threatened with bankruptcy. Several threads of the money trail were coming to dead ends in the internal audits. Sam wondered if Peter DeSantis knew where all the money was. *Maybe he did, and maybe that's why he's dead.*

As soon as the funeral was over, the news media stopped being respectful. There was, after all, both a murder investigation and rumors of pending financial catastrophe at a billion-dollar conglomerate.

Twenty-Three

Bloggers led the pack. They were by nature willing to write anything, especially the ones not based in Chicago. Some of them followed the murder investigation; some went sniffing on the money trail. The PR firm monitored everything they posted around the clock, and issued mild rebukes and corrections when necessary. Legal action could always be threatened, but that was held back when possible. The most scurrilous stuff was taken down by its authors. They got the message that all the spaghetti they were throwing at the wall was being watched.

The murder investigation was sexier than the money trail at this point, and there was room for speculation since the cops were being so stingy with the growing case file.

The DeSantis penthouse apartment in the John Hancock Center was sealed. Everything was photographed, even the stunning views of Lake Michigan that Peter DeSantis would have seen the instant before he died.

A few part-time staff at the Center provided some anonymous tidbits to the blogs, but the sources were quickly rooted out and fired. Discretion was part of the job description at Chicago's better addresses.

One of the real estate blogs estimated the penthouse's worth at $15 million, and wondered whether its value would go up or down based on its new notoriety as a crime scene. Not that it would be on the market anytime soon.

No surprise on the autopsy, which was quickly completed before the funeral. Cause of death was massive internal trauma caused by two close-range bullets. Police didn't say whether a silencer was used, but everyone assumed such a professional-looking hit had covered all the obvious bases. Chicago detectives were on the case, with probable cooperation from the FBI. DeSantis Industries was based in Chicago, but had many interstate and offshore relationships.

Oscar reassured the 63 DeSantis-funded Chicago community organizations that all financial commitments made by Peter DeSantis would be honored, even if not yet paid in full. The Chicago non-profit community started sleeping better, and said even nicer things about their benefactor than they had in the first round. Memorials to Peter DeSantis started sprouting on all their websites, usually as heartfelt personal reminiscences from their CEOs. It certainly didn't hurt to have the director of the Police Department's Widows' and Orphans' Fund say that Peter DeSantis had sent 100 kids to college, all expenses paid.

The bloggers also enumerated possible relationships between Peter DeSantis and Chicago organized crime. Outside of the usual labor union suspects, there wasn't much of a list. Chicago had grown into a very different city than it was during Al Capone's heyday. One of the more clever bloggers did an organizational chart of organized crime, with potential degrees of separation between each individual and Peter DeSantis. He clearly had too much time on his hands.

There was some examination of the history with Tony Addison, and the Addison Trucking merger that really put DeSantis Industries on the map. The Addison family wasn't biting. Their attorney said the Addison merger was old news, though reporters were certainly welcome to examine the records, if they wanted to take the trouble to find them. Tony Addison himself was getting on in years, and was not available to comment. The family lawyer wouldn't even disclose Tony Addison's whereabouts. He did dutifully record the contact information of every reporter who called.

Sam and Sandi were fascinated by the news coverage, especially the speculation on financial misdealings and potential bankruptcy. Reading the mostly off-base coverage was far more interesting than reviewing the endless boxes of records at the Fishbein office.

Sam wondered when his life as a double agent would be kicking in. So far, all he was hearing about were funeral arrangements and Oscar's day-to-day concerns about holding everything together at DeSantis Industries. Sam was a good soldier, and not only efficiently performed whatever Oscar asked, but tried to anticipate the needs of Fishbein's remaining named partner.

It was Sam's idea to interview Bernice, the housekeeper of Peter DeSantis and the last person to see him alive. Sam thought he'd be able to accompany his boss and participate in the questioning, but Oscar wanted to go alone. He had the DeSantis driver take him to Bernice's house in the Chicago neighborhood of Oak Park. Oscar had known Bernice for years, but had never been to her house. As he expected, she lived in a tidy house on an immaculate street.

Oscar hugged Bernice as soon as she opened the door. "My dear, I'm sorry I wasn't able to spend more time with you at the funeral," he said.

"That's fine, Mr. Sampson," Bernice said. "You had a lot of other things to do. By the way, your eulogy was wonderful."

"Thank you," he said. "How are you holding up?"

"It's been an awful time," she said. "Why would anyone want to kill him?"

"There are a lot of people trying to figure that out," Oscar said.

"Well, the detectives were very nice," Bernice said. "I'm sorry I didn't have more to tell them. I just kept the place clean, which wasn't too hard with someone as neat as Mr. DeSantis."

"You certainly did a wonderful job, and I wanted you to know that you will continue on the payroll just as you were," Oscar said. "I thought you might want to take some time off."

"I'm a pretty tough old lady," Bernice said, "but I might take you up on that."

"You are part of the DeSantis family, and I hope you know you can call me if there's ever anything you need."

"Thank you, sir, I really appreciate that," Bernice said.

"Please don't call me 'sir,' Bernice. Oscar is just fine."

"Okay, Oscar, thanks again."

Oscar stood to leave, and once more they hugged.

"Will you be going back to the penthouse any time soon?" she asked.

"I would like to, just to make sure all his papers are in order, but I'll wait until things simmer down a bit," he said.

"Well," she said, wanting to repay Oscar's generosity. "The detectives didn't really touch anything. They said there wasn't much for them to do. Everything is just the way he left it."

"Thank you, Bernice," Oscar said. "That makes me feel better."

Twenty-Four

Fishbein's bankruptcy preparations for DeSantis Industries stayed on track, with security even more intense than before. Sandi reported from New York that the Matriarchs were often seen hovering, and asking Robert for continuous progress reports. No one had to be reminded that consequences would be immediate and severe for any team member caught leaking information to any outsider. Some reporters did try calling both Fishbein's Chicago office and New York headquarters, but got nowhere.

Sam and Sandi communicated their official business via Fish Fone, usually sending copies of e-mails to Robert so that he'd be reassured, and could in turn reassure the Matriarchs. Their more interesting conversations were saved for their now-frequent late-night cell phone calls.

"Have you noticed that not one of the reporters has asked the most basic question?' Sam said. He was tired, back at his Chicago hotel room after a long day at Oscar's side. Sandi had called as soon as he walked in the door.

"Well, so far the reporters are looking at the surface stuff: how Peter DeSantis spent his money, how nice of an apartment he had, how nice he was to his people. What other question should they be asking?" Sandi asked.

"Who had a motive to kill him?" Sam stated flatly.

"Do you think it's someone connected to Addison Trucking?"

"I doubt it. That deal was cut years ago. If Tony Addison had felt burned, he would've taken action before now."

"Who else?" she asked.

"It's hard to come up with suspects here in Chicago. I've lost count of the number of people who tell Oscar how much they loved Peter DeSantis."

"Maybe this whole thing is just an enormous case of too much debt, and there is no smoking gun."

Sandi realized her mistake as soon as she said it. Of course there was a smoking gun. It had been used to kill Peter DeSantis.

She decided to change the subject: "How are things going at home?"

"We're playing a very frustrating waiting game," Sam said. "More chemo, which makes Theresa feel sicker, but it does keep the leukemia levels down and prevents more damage. My Mom is spending all her time at the hospital, praying for the right donor to show up. She's been crying during our phone calls lately, and all I can do is listen."

"What are the odds of finding a match?"

"There are more than 10 million people listed on the global registry, but it's a needle-in-a-haystack thing. There are a lot of different factors they look for, and the process can take weeks or even months before a donor can be found and a transplant scheduled."

"That is frustrating."

"Yeah, we keep losing the lottery. Theresa gets a rare form of breast cancer. She's one of the few who then develop leukemia. She doesn't respond well to the leukemia treatment. And her overeducated little brother isn't a worthy match for a bone marrow transplant."

"I checked the websites, Sam. Most family members are not suitable donors. Something like 70 percent don't match."

"Don't you think it's about time that someone catches a break around here?" he asked.

The Matriarchs had no intention of letting anyone catch a break. Oscar Sampson was a little untouchable at the moment, but everyone else was fair game. And Robert did his best to extract as much information as possible from Sam about Oscar's activities.

"What's on Mr. Sampson's schedule today?" read Robert's 7:30a.m. Fish Fone e-mail. Seven-thirty in New York was six-thirty in Chicago. Sam was about to hop into the shower, and figured he could wait awhile before responding. Robert hadn't called, just sent an annoying e-mail. Like most people, Robert was easier to deal with in person, or on the phone, than via e-mail. He had better manners when he was actually talking to you.

While Sam had been on the phone the night before with Sandi, she hadn't mentioned the latest DeSantis document she was working on, a routine scheduling item from one of the subsidiaries she was examining at Robert's direction. It shouldn't have been a big deal, but someone had apparently decided otherwise.

Sam got out of the shower and dried off, with a pithy response to Robert's first e-mail drafted in his head, including a thoughtful bit of humor to characterize all the housekeeping chores he was currently performing for Oscar. But, by the time he picked up the Fish Fone to respond to the first morning e-mail, the second one had already appeared.

This was one addressed to Sandi, but Sam was copied. So it was a message that Robert, obviously acting on behalf of the Matriarchs, wanted them both to hear.

"Big problem," it said. "Scheduling memo sent to entire DeSantis team. Sensitive information, not for all eyes."

Sam didn't know what the hell Robert was talking about. Sandi had sent out a scheduling memo yesterday, in addition to about 30 other e-mails she had sent related to the DeSantis project. They were nailing her about a scheduling memo?

For her part, Sandi felt sick, literally. She'd told Sam on their call the night before that she wasn't feeling well, that her stomach hurt. They both agreed it was probably stress, and she should try to get some sleep.

Sandi woke up feeling even worse. In addition to the stomach cramps, she also had a headache that didn't improve even after taking a couple of Tylenol. Since she was overdue for a doctor's checkup anyway, she called a quick-care health clinic. The nurse told her they had an opening and she should come right in.

Sandi was in the clinic's waiting room, hoping to make it into the office before anyone noticed, when Robert started in with more crazy, nagging e-mails. The scheduling memo he was now calling a "big problem" was one he had reviewed himself the day before. He had told Sandi to send it out to the DeSantis working group, which included the Fishbein lawyers and some DeSantis in-house counsel. It was really no big deal, and consisted of information that anyone could've acquired just by calling one of the secretaries. Sandi had put the smaller pieces together, at Robert's specific suggestion, sent it to him multiple times for his review, then sent it out. Along with many other e-mails that day, one of 30.

With her stomach cramping and her head hurting, Sandi watched the escalating messages from Robert, which not only copied Sam but also one or more of the Matriarchs.

Robert's "big problem" e-mail received a reply from Matriarch Mindy, noting her "concern," and copied several other people.

Matriarch Connie chimed in that "this is just the kind of thing we especially need to avoid during this sensitive time," and copied several other people.

Matriarch Carol said, "We need to fix this immediately," and copied several other people.

Then Matriarch Mindy doubled back, saying "I'm more concerned than ever," and copied Matriarch Laura. Sandi's stomach and head were pounding as the nurse came to take her into the doctor's office. The Fish Fone had almost frozen into her hand.

The doctor agreed that it was probably stress and lack of sleep.

Sandi didn't have the right answers when the doctor asked about her diet, either. Like many new associates during a crunch time, she was taking care of business but not taking very good care of herself.

Sandi laughed out loud when the doctor told her she should get some sleep, eat some soup, and stay home from work for a few days. She asked him for Xanax for the anxiety and Ambien to get some sleep. The quick-clinic doctor, who dealt with women like Sandi every day in his practice, gave her a small, non-refillable prescription for the anti-anxiety medication, and a refillable one for the sleep drug. He didn't want her to get hooked on Xanax, but he could see that she needed ongoing help to sleep with the kind of job she had.

Sandi confirmed the doctor's diagnosis when she asked for samples of both products. "I'm frankly not sure when I'll be able to get to a pharmacy to get these filled," she said. "Maybe after work tonight."

"I can give you enough to get you through the day," he said. "I assume taking the day off is not an option." One more time, Sandi laughed out loud. The doctor just nodded, and handed her the prescriptions and samples.

"Did you eat anything today?" was his closing line.

"No, but I'm going to get some yogurt and fruit right now," she said. And she did, grabbing both at the corner convenience store, before hailing a cab back to Fishbein, Schindler, Rose and Sampson.

In the 10-minute taxi ride, Sandi tried to think it through. She wanted to call Sam, but didn't. He was a time zone away in Chicago, and she wanted to handle this situation like the educated, professional woman she was and aspired to be.

So after wolfing down a small container of yogurt and a banana, she considered her options. They were, at best, limited.

The conflict over the scheduling document was a sham; she knew that. She could retrace her steps, document everything, and demonstrate to Robert that she had acted entirely within the instructions he had provided. He told her to write the memo. He told her what to include. He reviewed it at each step of the way. He told her to send it out. It would take some time to produce a timeline of everything that happened, but she could do it.

It would be a waste of time. Sandi couldn't go to Robert and the Matriarchs and refute all the "problems." They would just tell her that she had horribly misunderstood Robert's direction. They would tell her that they were concerned that she "just wasn't getting it." They would question her dedication as a team player at this difficult time.

The Matriarchs have all the power, she thought. Sandi and the other associates were the subordinates. Her still-hurting stomach and head told her she was right, and they were wrong, but it didn't matter. *Challenging them would only make things worse.* She had to suck it up and get through the day.

Sandi was about to text a message of apology for her misunderstanding of the situation, and any problems it may have caused, with helpful suggestions for next steps she could take to move the entire situation forward. But as she sat in the back seat of the taxi typing, her Fish Fone started flashing with yet another incoming message from Robert.

As Sandi paid the cab fare and headed into Fishbein's headquarters, she was transfixed by another unfolding mini-drama on her Fish Fone. She bumped into two people in the lobby, who were busy reading their own mini-dramas on their own Fish Fones. Who could count the number of these manufactured dramas going on in corporate America at any given time?

"Unfortunately, we seem to have another BIG problem," he texted.

Sandi got through security, up the elevator, and rushed to the DeSantis team's work area. She decided to short-circuit the next wave, and go right to Robert's office. Enough was enough.

But the door was closed and the lights were off in Robert's office. Nobody had seen him yet today. He was somewhere else, inflicting all this pain from the Matriarchs by remote control.

Sandi sat down at her cubicle and booted up her computer. She wished Sam were in the cubicle next door, at least for moral support and a friendly face.

Right now, all she could do was wait. And, gulp down one of the precious Xanax samples provided by the doctor.

Twenty-Five

Sam felt sorry for Sandi. He hadn't even responded to Robert's question about Oscar's schedule that day. He just watched the escalating e-mails describing one "big" yet completely illogical problem, then another.

Sometimes when you're sinking and wondering if it's your fault, it's good to be reminded that you're not crazy … and that it's really them, not you. Sam picked up his personal cell phone and called hers. He didn't want to take any unnecessary risks by using the Fish Fone.

"Sounds like you're in hell," he said after she instantly answered his call. "Did you make it to the doctor?"

"This whole thing kicked in when I was sitting in the clinic's waiting room."

"Great, the Matriarchs with a side dose of antibiotics." His attempt to make her laugh didn't work. She didn't respond at all. "How do you feel?" he finally asked.

"Well, the doctor gave me something to take the edge off."

She was actually a little groggy, but enough edge remained that she still wondered if she was to blame in some way for this morning's barrage. "I sent out 30 e-mails yesterday. They picked an innocuous one, and just started batting it around, right? Isn't that just nuts?"

"Yes, it's totally nuts. And you can't really defend yourself, because that would start a conversation you don't want to have," Sam said.

"I know, it would be a complete loser. So now I'm faced with probably having to apologize when I didn't do anything wrong." Her tone was defensive, and Sam could feel it, even 1,500 miles away.

"I know this won't make you feel any better, but it's how they operate. It's all about keeping you in your place, and trying to reinforce their position."

"Their position looks pretty solid to me," she said. "Why another attack?"

He decided it was time to tell her more. "Sandi, you know they're gearing up against Oscar. They probably did the same thing with Albert Rose."

"No kidding," she said.

"There's more. Oscar asked me to help him. Work for him, and work covertly against them. I agreed."

"What does that mean?" Sandi asked, rubbing her forehead. "How can you work both sides?"

"Well, so far I think that they don't know that I know that Oscar is trying to foil them." It was admittedly a mouthful. "And I'm pretty sure they don't know that he's recruited me to help him do more than DeSantis due diligence."

"Well, since you're willing to tell me that, I'm willing to tell you this: the Matriarchs asked me to keep an eye on you," she said. "That was the main point of our Girls' Lunch."

"No kidding?" Sam asked. So much for out-foxing the Matriarchs. Not to mention dodging a blue Buick in Midtown Manhattan.

"No kidding. So, what else are you up to?"

"Not much, at least not yet. The murder of Peter DeSantis has thrown off their battle plan, and I think both sides are recalibrating. That would explain why the Matriarchs are smacking you around, just to make sure you remain loyal to them."

"But what they're doing is kind of mean."

"It's more than kind of mean. It's mean, period." *And probably deadly*, he thought.

"And they've done it before."

"Of course, they've done it before. And it worked. Look at Robert."

"Wicked way to run a business," Sandi said.

"Also a lucrative way. They're at the top of the heap, and we both competed to join them."

"Bullshit," she said. Perhaps the Xanax had lowered her conversational inhibitions with Sam, but she meant it. "Aggressive legal tactics are one thing. Treating people like disposable chess pieces is something else."

"Hey, you're talking to a boy from the Midwest," he laughed. "We believe in being nice."

He managed to get a mild chuckle out of Sandi on that one. Probably a smile too, but he wasn't there to see it. Given what she'd already endured today, he considered it an achievement.

"Any idea what Robert's next BIG problem is all about?" Sam asked.

"No idea, but he's not even in the office," Sandi replied.

"Well, I spent last weekend on standby for these folks," he said. "I got through it, and as soon as they forget about this one, or are reassured by your continuing devotion, it'll blow over."

"That means I'm stuck until it blows over. Until I can make nice."

"Well, we're all kind of stuck that way," he thought. *Just keep dodging the blue Buicks.*

Sam was talking with Sandi on his personal cell phone, but the Fish Fone wasn't too far away in his room. He'd been using the Fish Fone to keep an eye on all the bouncing e-mails.

Suddenly, his Fish Fone screen went dark.

"Hey, did something just happen to the firm's e-mail?" Sam said, shaking the portable device. "My Fish Fone just died."

"No, my desktop computer is fine, and so is my Fish Fone," Sandi said. "Did you plug yours in overnight to recharge the batteries?"

"I thought so, but let me try again."

Sam started fumbling with the AC adaptor for the Fish Fone. He was pretty sure he'd let it charge overnight, but it was worth a shot.

Nothing.

"Sandi, is there a phone number for technical support? I'll try calling them from my room."

Sandi found the number, and Sam dialed. He got a recording. He left an urgent-sounding message.

"Do you want me to try for you?" she offered.

Sandi also got the recording when she called. She left another urgent message for the wizards in technical support, noting that her colleague in Chicago could not communicate, and that he was working on a vitally important project.

She also tried sending an e-mail on Sam's behalf to the Fishbein Help Desk. The associates had been told that if they ever had a problem, no matter where in the world they were, staff were on duty to help. Just an e-mail or phone call away. Twenty-four hours a day; seven days a week; 365 days of the year. It was understood that e-mail was the life line of the corporate world.

But not today. Not for Sam. No response.

"What do you think is going on?" she asked him.

"It could just be a computer thing," Sam rationalized. "Machines have moods, just like people do. Maybe the e-mail servers are having a bad day."

"But you're the only one who's affected. And no response from the computer guys."

Sam had to admit she was right. "Why would the Matriarchs cut me off?"

"You're talking to me?" she asked. "How does it feel, Sam?"

J.D. FOX

Twenty-Six

"I'd like to call this meeting of 'The Old Girls Club' to order," said Laura Henderson, with a slight smirk. The other four Matriarchs met her glance, and offered small acknowledgments of their own. Anyone entering the room would have sensed they shared a common bond, if only because of the matching square-cut blue diamonds on each woman's right hand.

Unlike Oscar Sampson and other male partners, they didn't stage their strategy meetings at fancy old restaurants. They were too busy to leave the building. The Matriarchs simply commandeered one of the nicest conference rooms at Big Fish headquarters, and had the in-house caterers deliver. Small salads, usually.

Still, this strategy meeting was different. The Fishbein Matriarchs had dealt with other suspicious deaths during their tenure – notably the named partners David Schindler and, most recently, Albert Rose. On top of that, a long-time client was the victim of a homicide, and the last remaining named partner was staying at arm's length in Chicago. Not good.

"Let's not forget we have a business to run, and a lot of mouths to feed," said Laura. "We'll get to our current dilemma in a minute, but let's do a quick check of our business units first."

The other Matriarchs had provided these reports before. They knew Laura Henderson wanted a quick overview of their areas of responsibility, with all the gloss removed. The reason this firm ran as well as it did was the direction from the top was always consistent and concise. And always focused on the bottom line. Laura kept tabs on everything, and she always knew what was what. This meeting was to pump up their collective confidence as much as anything else.

Carol, the Matriarch of Finance, went first. "Our revenue position remains strong," she said. "In fact, our prospects in Asia have never looked better."

Laura assumed Asia was being taken care of. She knew Europe was fine too. Lots of mergers and acquisitions on both continents. Fishbein was always first in line for multinationals that wanted to marry other multinationals, and had recruited aggressive regional directors to maintain the flow.

"Our biggest financial concern is one time zone away," Laura said. Everyone knew she meant the Central Standard Time Zone, specifically Chicago.

Carol nodded in agreement.

"Case management is strong, too," said Matriarch Mindy. "As of last night's tally, our partners, associates, and even our contract workers are billing at or above our projections for this month."

"Except that our projections beyond this month assume a very complicated and very time-consuming restructuring at DeSantis," said Laura, nailing the hole in Mindy's projections.

Mindy shrugged her Armani-suited shoulders. Laura was always right.

Matriarch Connie, who recruited both Sam and Sandi, along with the cream of every other top law school, was up next. "If you're wondering whether there's any talk at the law schools about the losses of our named partners, and the murder of a primary client, the answer is … of course … yes," she said, almost biting her lip.

"How do you know that?" asked Laura.

"There's some news coverage beyond Chicago. But mostly it's the law school student blogs. There's a couple of them at each law school. We monitor them every day. Fishbein rumors have been spiking."

"Go on, what's out there?" Laura asked.

"Some of the students speculate about the relative health of their prospective employers. Our latest financials and deal volume are always noted, but that's not as sexy as the passing of a named partner and a primary client."

All of the Matriarchs nodded when the collective deaths of Albert Rose and Peter DeSantis were referred to as "the passing." But they were all too smart to take any real comfort in it.

"And then, there's all the Twitter traffic," Connie said. "Students in law school seminars aren't very discreet, and they're making a lot of jokes in reference to the 'Big Fish and the Dead Mobster.'"

"Lovely, some sort of tired 'Swimming With the Fishes' thing?" Laura asked.

"Apparently the study of law doesn't fully occupy the students' time," Connie replied. "Of course, it never did, even back when I was on campus."

"All right, so in addition to our partner and client problems, we have a public relations problem, especially with our long-term student prospects." said Laura. "Are we keeping track of who's saying what so the offenders can be blocked from employment here?"

"Many students try to shield their real identities online, but we'll see what we can do," Connie said. Another project for the website wizards. They were good at this kind of thing.

"Thank you," Laura asked, turning to the Director of Marketing and Business Development. "Sarah, what do you think?"

"We're at or near the top of every published law firm ranking, including Chambers, Thomson, DealMaker, you name it," said Sarah, looking down at her square-cut diamond. She was the newest Matriarch, and obviously didn't feel as secure in her position as the others. Especially not when there were real problems to face. Sarah pulled a linen handkerchief from her purse, and quickly blew her nose.

"Right, top of the heap, our consistent position for more than a decade," said Laura. "What are the risks going forward, and what do you think we should do?"

"Promote our deals, our clients, our firm's culture, our pro bono work, and stay alert for positive publicity opportunities," offered Sarah, a canned PR response that would not be enough for this circle under these circumstances.

"Is anyone of significance working on stories about us, beyond reporting about the DeSantis murder itself?" asked Laura, cutting through Sarah's PR fog.

"Not that we know of, but of course we're monitoring."

Sarah was anointed a Matriarch after one of her staff scored an amazingly positive story in *The American Lawyer* titled, "How Fishbein Does It," that had been endlessly reprinted and included in every promotional package Fishbein sent to anyone. Her track record had been lean since her promotion. Sarah had been looking for a new way to impress the other Matriarchs.

"And do we coordinate our public messaging at all with Oscar Sampson, who is the go-to person for any reporter dealing with the Chicago situation?" asked Laura.

"Unfortunately," said Sarah, "Oscar Sampson pretty much does what he wants, although you've got to give him credit for how he's handled things so far. They love him in Chicago."

"I just talked with him, and frankly I don't find that of much comfort," said Laura, "not to mention his recent mishap in Midtown traffic." Looking right at Sarah, she said, "anyone care to enlighten the group on that one?"

The other Matriarchs were silent. Sarah again looked down at her pale blue diamond ring. After glancing in turn at each of the women in the room, Laura reached over to the telephone. An operator picked up the line instantly. "Can you send Robert in?"

For a few short moments, nothing more was said. Laura took a quick look at her Fish Fone, but no one else had brought theirs to this strategy meeting. It was a sign of respect for Laura, not to mention an acknowledgment of her unquestioned leadership of the Matriarchs.

Carrying a legal pad and a number of files, Robert lurched into the room. Glancing first at Sarah, he took a chair on the outer perimeter of the room. He was in the room, but not at the table.

All the Matriarchs turned to look at him. Robert's left hand started to shake a bit, which always happened to him when he was put on the spot. He tried to cover by adjusting his wire-rimmed glasses.

"If you don't mind, I'll skip the usual pleasantries," Laura began, more a prosecuting attorney than the paralegal she was trained to be. "Tell me the current status of DeSantis."

Robert thought for a moment to lighten the mood by saying, "He's still dead," but decided against it. No one at the table was in a laughing mood.

"Do you mind if I offer a blunt assessment?" Robert asked, which made him sound a lot more confident than he usually appeared.

"We'd appreciate it," Laura said.

"Oscar Sampson has gone 'rogue,' by which I mean he's doing what he wants, and not responding to any of the inquiries I have regularly left for him at the Chicago office and his hotel. He doesn't carry a Fish Fone."

Matriarch Sarah nodded at Robert, hoping his assessment of Oscar would vindicate hers. But Robert didn't make the mistake of saying that Oscar was doing a pretty good job of it, which of course no one at this table wanted to hear.

"What about the others?" asked Laura.

"His preferred associate is Sam Mitcham, and we're doing

our best to keep Mitcham in line," said Robert, explaining the blackout on Sam's e-mail and Fish Fone. "We have a pretty good lid on the personnel working on this account in the New York office. Unfortunately, we can't say as much for Chicago. Oscar Sampson has everything going through him, and he's trying to ignore us."

"Thank you Robert, that was blunt but it was just what I needed to hear," said Laura, with a nod. Robert knew he was being dismissed, and quickly darted out of the conference room. He could catch up with Sarah later. He was as anxious to please Laura, Mindy, Carol and Connie as she was.

Laura folded her hands, and lowered her head to meet them. She was thinking, and thinking hard. After a time, she looked back up. The other four Matriarchs were waiting for her analysis and decision.

"Well, this isn't the first time that we've dealt with one of our named partners behaving in a manner inconsistent with our long-term strategy," said Laura. Mindy, Carol, Connie and Sarah all nodded in agreement.

"What's next?" said Carol, speaking for the rest of the group.

"I think it's time for me to go to Chicago," said Matriarch Laura.

Twenty-Seven

Oscar Sampson wouldn't be immediately available to meet with Laura in Chicago. He had one of the DeSantis drivers taking him to Milwaukee for a lunch date with an old friend.

Oscar and Barbara Mitcham had been talking on the phone, but hadn't seen each other in quite awhile. He offered; she accepted. For her, it would be a nice break from the waiting game she and Theresa continued to play at the hospital.

The owners of Bacchus, often called the best restaurant in Milwaukee, were thrilled to hear from Oscar Sampson, and more than happy to reserve the corner table for his arrival. The restaurant, in the Cudahy Tower literally across the street from Lake Michigan, served fine Wisconsin cuisine at prices more familiar in Chicago or New York than in Milwaukee. Oscar always got the best, and shared it whenever he could. Today he was treating his old friend Barbara Mitcham.

Barbara visited Theresa at the hospital early in the morning, then went home to get ready.

She prided herself on appearing much younger than 60, her real age. Looking in the mirror, she realized the strain of the past several months was starting to show. There were a few wrinkles she hadn't seen before. But, as Barbara quickly reminded herself, she hadn't really looked in the mirror at all lately, beyond just taking a glance as she ran a brush through her hair. Her time was spent in the hospital's bone marrow transplant unit. Appearances didn't seem to matter much there. Many of the residents didn't even have hair on their heads, with many learning to shave in advance of the chemotherapy. Better than watching it fall out in clumps.

On the drive downtown, Barbara Mitcham also realized she hadn't paid much attention to the car lately. It wasn't filthy, but it wasn't clean either. At least the gas tank was half full. Or half empty. Barbara wasn't sure whether "half full" or "half empty" would describe her life right now. Here she was, a widow now for five years. With a son struggling with an intense job at a law firm. With a daughter enduring breast cancer, then leukemia, now waiting for a bone marrow donor. She said prayers for both of her children every day.

Oscar was waiting for her at the restaurant. Every bit a gentleman of the old school, he would never think of keeping a lady waiting. The lunch began with the warm embrace of old friends, and Oscar helped Barbara into her chair.

"You look very well," he said. "Always the prettiest girl in the room."

"And you," Barbara smiled. "Always the smartest man in the room, often the most charming."

"How are you holding up?" they said to each other, almost in unison.

"I'm holding steady," said Oscar. "Let's talk about you and your family."

The sincerity in Oscar's wise eyes, not to mention their personal history, brought Barbara to tears. She almost immediately caught herself, and swallowed hard.

"It's been very difficult," she finally managed to say.

"Are you satisfied with the quality of Theresa's care?" Oscar asked.

"Yes, we're fine there." she said. "I appreciate everything you and Peter DeSantis tried to do." Barbara didn't mean to make a reference to Oscar's dead friend and major client, and continued, almost in a whisper, "Oh, Oscar, I'm so sorry for everything that's happened ... I know how much he meant to you."

Oscar smiled warmly and nodded. He was unfortunately well-versed at hearing words of condolence about Peter DeSantis.

"Anyway, I've received phone calls from doctors and hospital executives all over the country," Barbara said. "That was very thoughtful of you both."

"Most of that was Peter's idea," said Oscar. "Could anyone offer to help?"

"Not the kind of help we need," she replied. "Theresa is at one of the best facilities in the country. Her doctors are terrific. Her nurses are amazing."

"What she needs is a donor," Oscar stated.

"What she needs is a donor," Barbara agreed.

"There's an international registry of donors," Oscar said. "Nothing there?"

"Nothing there yet," she said. "And the clock is ticking."

"Sam was so disappointed that he wasn't a match. He's quite a remarkable young man. Reminds me a lot of both you and his father."

"Poor Sam," his Mom said. "He lost his father before he could become a man himself."

"I think he's well on his way to becoming a fine man," Oscar said.

Oscar's words reminded Barbara that both of her children were in trouble, though she hoped the "life-threatened" status applied only to Theresa. "Sam and I still talk almost every day on the phone, as we have since Larry died. Sam hasn't been saying much about work."

"As I said, things are holding steady," Oscar said.

The food came and went. Barbara and Oscar picked at steak salads. They hadn't seen each other lately, but they'd been in each others' lives so long that there wasn't a constant need for small talk.

Oscar had come to lunch with this dear old friend with an agenda. Not the agenda of a powerful lawyer intent on making a deal for the best possible price. The agenda of a powerful man who was willing to do almost anything to benefit a true friend.

"Barbara, I think it's time we talk about the other potential donor for Theresa."

Barbara gasped. She immediately knew what he meant, and now understood why he was here in person. "Oscar, that was more than 40 years ago. I wouldn't know where to begin."

"Actually, that *was* the beginning for me," Oscar said. "You and Larry were still in high school, and I was in college, just thinking of going to law school."

Barbara remembered easily. "Larry and I were so scared. We were in love, we were in high school, and we weren't ready to have a baby."

"You were able to have two babies, later, when you *were* ready," Oscar said, repeating his warm smile.

The wheels immediately began turning in Barbara's head. What happened 40 years ago was now very relevant.

"When we gave the baby up for adoption, we agreed that we would never have contact with him."

"Yes, that was the typical arrangement back then."

"And the adoption records were sealed."

"That was also the arrangement back then."

Barbara had two bites of steak salad left on her plate. Her appetite was gone, and she put down her fork.

"Oscar, Theresa and Sam don't know they have a brother. Larry never told them. I never told them. No one has ever told them."

"They don't necessarily need to know," Oscar replied. "But Theresa needs a donor, and isn't another male sibling the best potential match?"

Barbara was glad she'd stopped eating. At the moment, she was having trouble breathing.

"Oscar, do you know where he is?"

Oscar Sampson, who had spent a lifetime covering every angle to deliver the best possible deal for his clients, nodded.

"I have a couple of people working on it. With your permission, we're going to make contact."

Barbara Mitcham, who placed her trust in Oscar Sampson 40 years ago before anyone else knew just how talented he was, looked straight into his eyes, and said: "Yes, please."

Twenty-Eight

Sam's Fish Fone came back to life, almost with a lurch.

The red light started flashing immediately. First there was an incoming pile of messages which had accumulated since he got cut off. At the top of the list, a new urgent message from Robert that Laura was in Chicago and wanted to see him.

The Midwest headquarters of Fishbein, Schindler, Rose and Sampson were right on Chicago's Loop. They occupied the top ten floors of a very nice, very expensive corporate office building. Law firms always took the top floors.

Since Chicago was a major airport hub, many domestic Fishbein personnel worked there temporarily while in the Midwest or, for the offshore lawyers, in the United States. A lot of international business moved through Chicago. It was often cheaper to do a big deal in Chicago than in New York.

Fishbein's Chicago office had a whole wall of temporary offices available for the visitors. Oscar Sampson always got the nicest one, in the corner, when he was in town. Matriarch Laura could also command her choice of temporary office space. Sam and the other associates took whatever was left.

Word spread quickly that Laura was coming to Chicago. Robert was thoughtful enough to alert the maintenance staff, who set up a temporary office especially for her. A bud vase of white roses was waiting on her desk, just the way she liked it.

Sam was up and into the office early anyway, and got his usual mid-hall office. It had a window with a view of the building next door, but with a few of the nicer secretaries outside the door. One of them pointed out Laura's temporary digs, and Sam hustled down for what he was sure would be a difficult meeting.

The office was empty. No Laura, no signs of occupancy. Just fresh white roses on the desk.

Sam went back to his office, and e-mailed Robert. No response.

Once again, they've got me in standby mode, he thought. That would end soon enough. In the meantime, he called Sandi on their personal cell phones.

"Hey, stranger," Sandi said on the first ring. "Still in Computer Hell?"

"I've been upgraded to Purgatory," Sam joked.

"And you're waiting to see Laura?"

"Word travels fast. What do you know?"

"Laura called a meeting of the Matriarchs. Robert was summoned. He left the conference room after a few minutes. I saw him meeting later with Sarah. No high-fives this time. They both looked serious. He's such a weasel."

"True, but just imagine the pain of being him," Sam said

"Looks like a safer career position than you or me."

"I know, but fuck 'em."

Sam never swore to Sandi before. It took her aback, but just for a moment.

"What are you going to say to Laura?" she asked.

"As little as possible."

"Where's Oscar? What does he say you should do?

"He's not around, and hasn't returned my calls. I'm on my own."

"You'll be fine. You can't answer questions you don't know the answers to."

"That's what I was thinking. I'll let you know how it goes."

"Gotta go, here comes Robert," Sandi said, hanging up.

Sam could hear a couple of short knocks on his office door. He had no time to react before Laura pushed open the door and walked in.

"Hi, Sam."

"Hello! Robert said you might be looking for me," was all Sam could think of to say.

"Walk with me," she said, and Sam detected what he thought was a slight curl on her lip. He immediately got up and followed her out the door, doing his best to hide the sudden spike in his blood pressure.

Laura led Sam right past the office set aside for her, down the hall, around the corner, into an empty conference room. She motioned him in, and closed the door behind them.

Nothing was said for a few moments. Sam and Laura sat down in two of the upholstered leather chairs.

"Sam, how are you?" she finally said, as she looked down to make a slight adjustment in her slate grey Chanel travel suit.

"I'm fine, how are you?" he said, already thinking it was a lame response, but knowing his job right now was to keep the ball in the air.

"Frankly, we're going through some hard times," she said, looking straight into his eyes.

"I assume you're referring to the deaths of Albert Rose and our Chicago client?" Sam asked, stating the obvious.

"That's bad enough, but I'm looking beyond that, Sam."

After a long pause, during which Laura again just stared into his eyes, Sam said, "How can I help?"

Laura, who had been running Fishbein a very long time, ignored the first year associate's attempt to deflect her. Sam suddenly felt as though he was completely outgunned, and it was all the more complicated because he didn't know where Oscar was, or what had been discussed between Oscar and

Laura. Laura was going around Oscar, directly to Sam.

"I'm going to be blunt with you, Sam."

"Please tell me what's on your mind."

Laura's face started to visibly flush and turned red. Sam couldn't tell if she was about to cry or yell at him.

"My job, Sam …" she began, then faltered. Sam just waited, trying not to show the terror he was starting to feel.

"My job," she said again, "My first job, is to protect this firm from harm. Right now, I sense we're under threat."

"From two homicide investigations?" Sam ventured.

She ignored his question. "Sam, wouldn't it be fair to say that you know everything there is to know about the DeSantis case?"

"I know a lot," he volunteered. "I know the case file, I know how complicated it is. I know there's a lot of money involved."

Laura cut him off. "It's not just the money, Sam. I know the numbers don't add up. But, more important than that, we're looking at the very real possibility of criminal liability. In the worst case scenario, this Chicago case could bring down our firm, and land us in jail."

Sam hadn't heard it put that way before. Criminal liability? He was mute.

"So I'd like to hear what you know," she said. "Of course, I'll also speak to Oscar, but as the Chief Operating Officer of this firm, I need you to give me a full briefing. You can start right now."

Sam cleared his throat. He was totally unprepared for a cross examination by Matriarch Laura.

"Before you begin, one other thing," she said.

"What?" he asked.

"I know all about Oscar Sampson's history with your mother. So don't try to bullshit me to protect him. You'd regret it."

Twenty-Nine

Theresa Mitcham would rush to protect her brother, if she had known he was being interrogated by the First Matriarch. She would have done the interrogating herself, if she had known about the meeting between Oscar Sampson and her Mom.

Instead, she was lying in a hospital bone marrow transplant unit, wondering if she was going to live or die.

Theresa Mitcham had never been one to feel sorry for herself, but in the current circumstances, she not only asked "why me?" but also "what next?"

Among her spare comforts were the nurses who hovered over her. There was no privacy on a bone marrow transplant (BMT) unit. There were simply too many things that could go wrong, and that would require immediate intervention. If anything happened, they were at her side immediately. Like the time she fainted in the bathroom.

Theresa was reminded of just how sick she was every time a nurse brought in a new batch of chemotherapy medication. Because chemo is so toxic, BMT nurses have to wear masks and gloves for their own protection. They hook up the clear plastic bags to one of the machines at the patient's bedside, input all the dispensing instructions on a bedside computer, and hook up the intravenous line to the patient. In Theresa's case, since she had to receive so many treatments so often, the doctors had surgically implanted a port into her chest to ease the infusions. The nurses didn't have to stick her with a needle, they just hooked the IV line to her port.

The process of receiving chemotherapy can take awhile. The whole bag of liquid doesn't go in all at once. It can take hours. And hours later, or maybe even a day later, the side effects kick in. Nausea, fatigue, fever, rashes, you name it. A lot of it just had to be endured, all in the hopes that it was keeping the leukemia at bay until a bone marrow match could be found.

Today's custom-mixed chemotherapy wasn't up from the pharmacy yet, so Theresa got a physical therapy session. Since she was confined to a hospital bed for so much of the time, it was important for her to exercise and maintain muscle tone. When she was strong enough, she would walk around the BMT unit corridors, wheeling an IV drip unit alongside her. On days like today, when she didn't have the energy to get out of bed, a physical therapist showed up to coax her.

"How are we feeling today?" said the PT in the light green smock, though of course she already knew the answer. She was wearing a nametag that said, *Gail*.

"I've been better," Theresa said. "Time to get this body moving a little?"

"Absolutely," Gail said, sliding onto the side of the bed, and helping Theresa into a sitting position. It was easier said than done, since there were a lot of tubes and monitors in the way. Theresa felt like hell, but was always cooperative. She knew everyone in the unit was there to help her.

The physical therapy was very light. Arms up, arms down, a bunch of times. One leg up, one leg down, a bunch of times. Something that looked a little like a yoga move, designed to maintain stability of the midsection. Gail wrote notes on everything they did.

But even very light physical therapy is taxing for a leukemia patient undergoing chemotherapy. Theresa started to sweat, and

Gail wiped her brow with a small towel.

"Do you have any muscle soreness?" Gail asked.

"My back is a little stiff," Theresa answered.

"Yeah, that will happen with so much time in bed. Let's do a few twists." Theresa had been through all these moves before, trained by Gail and the other therapists who worked at the BMT unit. She tried to do the moves on her own, but it was kind of like having a trainer at the gym – exercise happens more when there's someone watching and pushing you.

As the physical therapy continued, Theresa wondered where her Mom was. She knew about the scheduled lunch with Oscar Sampson, and hoped they were having a nice time. Along with everything she was enduring, it was tough to see the worry on her Mom's face, day in and day out. Lunch in downtown Milwaukee with an old friend should be a nice break. She'd be sure to ask what her Mom had learned about Sam's work drama. He hadn't offered much during their last few phone conversations.

Relative to everything else she was dealing with, physical therapy was a break for Theresa. It actually felt good.

Then the cart from the pharmacy arrived, containing Theresa's latest round of chemotherapy. Joan, one of Theresa's favorite nurses, came in the room. Gail eased her way out, with an admonition to Theresa to "keep it up."

Joan put on a protective gown, and then a face mask. A splash of the toxic mixture would easily burn her skin.

The chemotherapy ritual continued, with Joan and Theresa making small talk while Joan checked the port on Theresa's chest.

Today's medication, which was in a quart-sized clear plastic bag, was then placed on a rack above Theresa's head, so that gravity would help take the liquid down. Joan punched the day's dispensing instructions into the computer, and hooked up the line to Theresa's port.

The process was high-tech, but it wasn't flawless. Sometimes the computer started beeping, and needed to be reset. Sometimes the IV lines got twisted, and needed to be straightened out. Sometimes there was a leak, which made Joan glad she was wearing all the protective gear.

Theresa could see that everything was working, but she really couldn't feel the medication going into her. Once you get used to a port implanted into your chest, individual infusions don't faze you.

"Okay, you're all set," Joan said. "Press the call button if you need me." She went out the door to see another patient on the BMT unit.

Theresa looked at the monitors, at the bag of chemotherapy, and her eyes ran along the clear plastic pipeline feeding into her port. She felt tired now, and knew she'd feel much worse later.

Theresa Mitcham had been in medical limbo for more than a year. After aggressive breast cancer, then a lumpectomy, then leukemia, now she had to endure preparation for a bone marrow transplant and the search for a donor.

She wondered how much longer this could go on.

Thirty

"I've seen the expense records," said Laura. "You had some nice meals with Oscar and Peter DeSantis."

Laura and Sam remained in the nondescript Chicago conference room. A naked light bulb would've enhanced this interrogation scene, but this wasn't a movie. It was Sam's life, and he had a difficult role: find a way to placate Laura, without creating new problems for Oscar. So this was what double agents did for a living, Sam thought.

Sam remembered from law school that you can't libel the dead.

"So far as I could tell, Peter DeSantis very much set the tone for our firm's relationship with him," Sam began. "Business executives of his era did a lot of three-martini lunches."

"It's amazing to me that they were still standing after that much vodka," Laura said, almost smiling. *What was she up to?* Sam wondered.

"I didn't get to spend that much time in their company before the murder, but I'd have to say that he held his liquor pretty well."

"Yes, the murder," said Laura. "What a tragedy. And what curious timing, coming just as a giant restructuring was about to commence." *This,* thought Sam, *coming from a woman who presides over a firm where multiple partners died under suspicious circumstances.*

"It's certainly a complicated matter, when you take all the business operations and subsidiaries into account," said Sam.

Laura paused, and Sam decided to address her previous bombshell.

"I must admit that I don't understand your concern about criminal culpability," he said.

Just then, their conversation was interrupted by a brisk knock on the door. One of the Chicago secretaries stuck her head in. "Ms. Henderson, Sarah is on the line for you from New York."

Laura dismissed the interruption with a wave. "Let her know I'll talk to her later." She was much more interested in this discussion with Sam than with a call from one of the other Matriarchs.

She returned her gaze to Sam.

"I think there's more going on here than bad debt leading to a bankruptcy," Laura said. "You know the numbers don't add up."

"I know that we're looking at years of complicated financial transactions, and very sophisticated accounting," Sam offered.

"I think it goes way beyond that, and that's what worries me. You didn't get a sense of any of that over your three-martini lunches?"

"You're losing me, and as I said, there weren't that many lunches."

Sam thought for a second that now might also be the point to ask why the relationship between Oscar and his Mom might have any bearing on any of this, but he decided to play it as close to the vest as he could.

"I expected to do more listening than talking in this session, Sam."

"And I want to be helpful. I sincerely don't know where you're going with this."

Actually, he did have a sense of where Laura was going. He was hoping his young associate poker face would hold up.

"What do you know about DeSantis Industries' offshore accounts?" Laura asked.

Sam had to hand it to her – Laura was a smart woman. And he knew she'd probably spent a lot of time over the years cleaning up behind the partners of Fishbein, Schindler, Rose and Sampson.

"The records indicate a number of accounts in the Cayman Islands," said Sam.

"Exactly," Laura said. "How many accounts, and how large are they?"

"I haven't memorized the ledgers," Sam said, now feeling that he really was being interrogated. He decided to play the one other card he had: "Perhaps my mental capacity has been affected by that brush with the blue Buick."

"Excuse me?" Laura asked, momentarily thrown off course.

"Luckily, I was able to push Oscar out of the way," Sam said. "I ripped my suit jacket, but that was it."

Laura just stared at him. Sam was trying to concentrate on breathing *in and out, in and out.*

He was rescued by another tapping at the door, with another secretary looking in and saying, "Sarah in New York is on the line, saying she really needs to speak with you."

Laura was not in the mood. "Tell her I got the first message five minutes ago, was interrupted just now by the second message, and will call her back." The blood seemed to drain from the unfortunate messenger's face as she ducked back out the door.

"Now, where were we?" Laura asked, returning to Sam.

The interruption gave him a little time to get his bearings. "You were asking me more than I know about the offshore accounts of DeSantis Industries," he said. "Oscar can probably answer those questions for you much better than I could."

"And you can bet I'll be talking to Oscar. Where is he?"

"I'm afraid I don't know. He doesn't as a rule share his

schedule unless he has a specific request for me."

"God forbid one of our founding partners would actually stick to a schedule," she said, probably indicating more frustration to Sam than she really wanted him to hear. And for his part, he almost started to sympathize with Laura and appreciate the job she'd been doing all these years. Almost.

But Laura snapped Sam back to reality with her next question.

"Yes or no question, Sam. Do you know anything about DeSantis funds being illegally stashed outside the country?"

"No," said Sam. "I've never heard anything of the sort."

"That's where the criminal culpability comes in," she said. "Money laundering by a named partner could bring down the whole firm."

There was no time for Laura's explosive charge to sink in. A third secretary rapped on the conference room's door, for a third time.

"I have Sarah on the line from New York."

Laura didn't even bother addressing the third secretary. She grabbed the telephone extension and simply said, "What?"

Sam watched as Laura listened to Sarah from New York. The watching and listening continued for at least 30 seconds. Sam could see Laura's face reddening; it appeared she was coming to a boil.

"You interrupted me three times to tell me that?" she exploded. "Do you think this is building my confidence in your ability to handle a real emergency?"

Laura slammed down the phone and glared at Sam.

"I built one of the top firms in the world, and all I'm doing lately is cleaning up other people's messes," Laura said. "That'll be all for now."

Sam tried not to bump into the table or trip as he made a hasty exit.

He'd survived the interrogation, and could pass along two valuable bits of information to Oscar. First, Laura was suspicious about possible money laundering on the DeSantis account. Sam had wondered about that himself, and whether that's what Peter DeSantis meant by the "Chicago Way" of doing business.

Second, and probably at least as interesting to Oscar: there was at least one crack in the Matriarch's united front – Sarah.

Thirty-One

Sam didn't know where Oscar was, but had to tell someone about his meeting with Laura. He called Sandi on her personal cell phone. This was definitely not information to trust to the Fish Fones.

Sandi didn't answer. She was busy, about to face an interrogation of her own.

Robert called Sandi into his New York office at midday. He wanted to have a little chat, at Sarah's suggestion. Robert told her to grab coffee or something else to drink on her way. When she arrived at his door, she noticed an assortment of mini-cupcakes lined up on top of his desk.

She suppressed the urge to wince. Her goofball supervisor was making nice this time, and was probably calculating that the way to her heart, or her brain, was through her stomach!

"Hungry for some sugar?" Robert asked, with as sincere a smile as he could muster.

His transparent motives aside, Sandi remembered that she hadn't really eaten anything for breakfast, in spite of the doctor's admonitions to take better care of herself.

"I have red velvet with cream cheese frosting, double-chocolate, and yellow with pink butter cream frosting," Robert said, pointing at the baby cupcakes as he named them. "Please, help yourself."

Sandi accepted a double-chocolate cupcake, and took a bite. Then, a quick swallow of coffee. Then a pause, just to see what Robert would do next.

"I think it amounts to fewer calories if you just eat these small ones," Robert said, in almost passable small talk. "They're from the little bakery down the street."

"They're very good," Sandi said.

After another deliberate smile and a nod, Robert got down to business.

"What do we hear from our friends in Chicago?" he asked.

"They're busy, of course, just like everyone here," Sandi said, waiting for Robert to start drilling down.

"Our First Matriarch is there right now," he said, sounding almost conspiratorial. It was wasted breath on his part. Sandi could tell exactly what he was trying to do.

"That's what I heard," she said. "Are we expecting a significant development on the case?"

Robert didn't stage this little meeting to answer questions; he wanted to ask them. "I think Laura is concerned both with the big picture," he said, extending his arms to indicate breadth, "and also with the smallest details," he said, drawing his hands together. "In the big picture, we have a dead founding partner, a murdered client, a complicated restructuring, and a balance sheet that doesn't add up." Robert wasn't sharing any information. Everyone on the case knew about the layers and layers of problems.

"On top of that, the founding partner on the case hasn't been in regular contact, and doesn't acknowledge many of my messages to him," Robert continued. "Do you know anything about that?"

"No," Sandi said. "I haven't communicated with Oscar Sampson at all."

"And then, there's our friend Sam."

Sandi swallowed the last of her little chocolate cupcake. She knew Sam would be the real object of this conversation.

"The last I heard from him, he was having computer problems," she ventured.

"Yes, we took care of that," Robert said. Sandi knew Robert had ordered the blackout's start and stop, probably suggested by Sarah. Not very classy, but the look-who's-in-control-around-here message was clearly received.

"The impression I get is that Sam is even busier in Chicago than we are here in New York," Sandi said. "For us, DeSantis is our big case. In Chicago, it's also a local murder investigation."

"Has Sam revealed to you the detailed substance of his work for Oscar Sampson, beyond acting as his messenger boy?" Robert asked.

Sandi was momentarily grateful that Sam had not yet told her everything he'd learned about the case, because she was now able to truthfully tell Robert, "no, nothing more than he's written in his regular reports to you."

All that changed when this little session ended and Sandi got on the private line with Sam. After being reminded of what she was going through, he told her everything about his meeting with Laura. Everything he knew about the case. Everything about the near-miss with the blue Buick. And, everything he knew about Oscar Sampson and his mother.

It was also at this point that Sandi and Sam started referring to their DeSantis case supervisor as "Robert" only when they had to, to his face and on e-mail. Between the two of them, he would now be known simply as "Cupcake."

Thirty-Two

For the past two decades, most legal documents and government filings have been stored electronically, with elaborate back-up systems at law firms and government offices. There are even back-ups to the back-ups, filed on high-capacity disks and stored at undisclosed locations around the country.

It's a little different for legal matters going back into the 1950s. For those old deals and cases, there's a mountain of paper. Sometimes it's easy to find old records; sometimes it's not.

DeSantis Industries was built on many deals over many years. And, the deals were mostly done in Chicago. Peter DeSantis was an ambitious man in a hurry. An elegant paper trail was not his priority.

Still, just the *possibility* of a DeSantis restructuring had been keeping lawyers in both Chicago and New York busy for months. They pored over the electronic records of the last decade, and the boxes and boxes of paper.

Sam had been through all the boxes in Chicago, and Sandi had been through all of them in New York. There were a lot of boxes, but there could've been many more. Especially when it came to the Addison Trucking merger, the big deal that really made the company, the amount of paper was kind of sparse.

Sam was a regular enough presence at the Chicago DeSantis

offices that he was starting to make friends. The CEO's murder and funeral probably facilitated the sharing of secrets by the long-time DeSantis employees.

"Why isn't there more paper?" Sam asked one of the DeSantis accountants, a fifty-something guy named Arnie.

"That's just the way they did it back then," Arnie said. "Part of the plan." Arnie reached for a toy garbage truck on his desk.

"One of the many services provided by the old Addison Trucking Company was the 'Shred Sleds' unit," Arnie explained to Sam.

"Shred Sleds?" Sam asked.

"Here's how it worked," said Arnie. "Let's say a company was remodeling, and had to clean out the storeroom. It's stuffed with files no one has touched for years. There's probably some personnel or financial stuff in there, but it's so old that there's no chance anyone would need it," he explained.

"Nor was there any law saying it had to be kept forever," Sam added.

"Exactly," Arnie replied. "So, the prudent Chicago office manager would book a Shred Sled. They were popular, even made into little toys like this. Notice the two big compartments on the side."

"What are they?" Sam asked, examining the little Sled.

"Hydraulic shredders. One Shred Sled could go through a small roomful of old records in a few hours, and then cart away the shards to an incinerator," Arnie said.

"That's ingenious," Sam said.

"The Sleds were a big hit," Arnie said. "Especially in this city, where a few bad income tax returns sent Al Capone to prison, the idea that 'your business is no one else's business' really caught on."

"And, how cool is the toy version?" Sam asked. "I bet every Chicago kid wanted one."

"Well, I got free ones for my boys," Arnie said, with a smile. "And, since the Shred Sheds came to you, you didn't have to worry whether everything was really getting shredded," he added. "You could watch it work, and many people did. It was amazing to see how quickly a hydraulic shredder could go through a box of old files."

"Tony Addison never kept many records as he built his trucking business, did he? Sam asked.

"God, no," Arnie said. "There's an old story about that one."

"I figured there would be," Sam said.

Arnie put his feet up on his desk. This was so much more interesting than accounting. "Before he finally sold Addison Trucking Company to Peter DeSantis, the Shred Sleds were suddenly unavailable to outside customers."

"All booked up," Sam said.

"Tony kept them parked in his own giant garages. First, they shredded whatever was in all those old boxes – whatever records they *had* kept. Then, his boys burned the thin, shredded paper strips. They kept a few incinerators going for weeks."

"Addison was a careful and thorough man, just like DeSantis." Sam said.

"Like many of his customers, he supervised the shredding process personally," Arnie said.

They still remembered Tony Addison in Chicago, though no one had seen him for awhile. All the news coverage of the DeSantis murder brought him back to prominence for a new generation of Chicago residents. The stories would invariably throw up an old black-and-white photo of Tony from the '70s. With a sour expression and wearing a striped suit, the picture made him look like a Mafia boss – the kind of guy who could be involved in a murder.

The murder investigation was going cold. The crime scene had been immaculate, aside from the dead body of Peter DeSantis. In spite of all the intense media speculation, no real witnesses came forward. The bloggers breathlessly ran details on every sad sack who said his mother was related to a doorman at the John Hancock

Center, but none had a credible connection.

The news crews no longer parked outside the Center, waiting to record the comings and goings of every celebrity resident's personal assistant. The celebrities themselves were starting to come back too, though they all rode their limos into the basement and came up the inside elevators.

The penthouse apartment of Peter DeSantis remained vacant. A couple of cleaning crews went through – one provided by the John Hancock Center as a service to its residents, another provided by Oscar Sampson as a service to the neighbors. And to Bernice. Oscar wanted it in good shape when she got back from her time off. Assuming she'd be willing to go back up there.

The Hancock Center's security team politely turned away even the celebrity neighbors who wanted to take a peek. There were never any bullet holes in the walls to see, even on the day of the murder. The brunt force of the bullets was taken by Peter DeSantis himself, and a little to the leather executive chair he was sitting in at the time. The chair was discreetly disposed of, with Oscar's approval.

The Hancock Center's management fielded a lot of calls from Chicago's always-hungry real estate agents, checking to see if there was any possibility that the penthouse would be put on the market. All inquiries were politely declined, as Oscar had instructed. Estimated worth of the place was still thought to be about $15 million.

There were many millions more on the minds of the nonprofit organizations still supported by DeSantis Industries. Rumors bounced around that an umbrella foundation might be established to continue the good works of Peter DeSantis.

For now, at Oscar Sampson's explicit direction, every one of the 63 arts, cultural and health care groups favored by Peter DeSantis got paid. Every child of a fallen police officer or firefighter got this semester's scholarship check, as promised. Exactly as Peter DeSantis would have wanted, and would have expected of his dear friend and counsel.

Thirty-Three

As a seasoned and expert counsel himself, Oscar Sampson knew when to ask for help.

Oscar knew corporate law forwards and backwards. Specifically, Oscar knew the law and procedure of M&A – Mergers and Acquisitions. In fact, a lot of what was known in the field was originally dreamed up by Oscar and his partners Morris Fishbein, David Schindler, and Albert Rose. Their specialty was especially lucrative, and made rich men out of both the partners and their clients, including Peter DeSantis.

What Oscar didn't know, at all, was current child welfare and adoption law. He had implied to Barbara Mitcham that he and his team were on the verge of contacting her other son. Oscar wanted her blessing before he made any move whatsoever. Now that he had her consent, he needed the most seasoned expert he could find in child welfare law. And he wanted to move quickly.

Oscar knew that Jane Chapnick would take his call. They weren't exactly close friends, but he had supported her work with Mothers Need Lawyers from the start. Fishbein, Schindler, Rose and Sampson were charter members of her donor group, and were always listed prominently in the program for her annual fundraising galas. The firm also provided pro bono support whenever she needed it, and Jane Chapnick was never shy about asking when she needed the leverage of a huge law firm with deep pockets.

So much had happened since they last talked. For one thing, her star student, Sam Mitcham, had opted to work at the firm rather than taking the offer Jane had arranged at Mothers Need Lawyers. Right now, in spite of the paycheck Sam was drawing, his choice looked like a bad one. Who could have foreseen the death of named partner Albert Rose just before Sam was about to start work?

On top of that, Jane Chapnick read the law blogs and talked with law students every day. Fishbein was under a very dark cloud. The murder investigation involving a primary firm client was still active in Chicago. Said primary client, minus its murdered president and chief executive officer, was probably about to declare itself bankrupt and bust into a lot of little pieces. Restructuring was certainly a recognized specialty, but what about all those rumors of Chicago mob connections?

Then there was the matter of the Matriarchs. Jane Chapnick knew all the rumors of their alleged connection to the death of Albert Rose and all the unanswered questions about the deaths of the other named partners. She had heard the jokes that Fishbein had no mandatory retirement age, because it didn't need one.

Jane had been in regular direct contact over the years with the Matriarchs, especially the director of legal recruiting, Connie. Fishbein always recruited the cream of her crop, with an eye towards potential corporate hustlers. Jane Chapnick believed that a great lawyer was a great lawyer, she just had the ones with heart. Fishbein paid top dollar, and always provided real support to pro bono programs, which explained why students like Sam and Sandi picked the firm year after year.

"Oscar, it's been awhile!" Jane began, after their respective secretaries finally got them on the phone at the same time. "Are you calling from Chicago?"

"Jane, it's good to hear a friendly voice," Oscar replied.

And then, both because he was a gentleman and he was about

to request a big favor, he asked about everything going on in Jane's world. It was what she did all the times the roles were reversed, and she called to ask a favor of him.

Oscar also took care to compliment her star student, while leaving out the part about Sam being a double agent in his escalating battle with the Matriarchs.

"Sam is probably the brightest young man, and most capable young mind, I've ever encountered," Oscar said, adding, "he's the reason I'm calling you today."

"You know I'll do whatever I can," Jane said, before she even knew what Oscar would be asking.

Oscar told her about his history with Barbara and Larry Mitcham, how he had not only set them up on their first date, but was the friend they consulted when they got in trouble. He knew that their first son's name was Jacob.

"And this was a private adoption in Wisconsin almost 40 years ago, before you had a law license or even went to law school?" Jane asked.

"Yes, and I didn't save anything. We were told the records would be sealed, and that no contact would be permitted. I don't know where Jacob is, or if he knows he's adopted. I do know that there is a vital health concern motivating this contact."

Jane Chapnick put her hand over the receiver, and told her Columbia Law School assistant to cancel her next meeting and hold all calls. This was going to take awhile.

Oscar then told Jane about Theresa's leukemia, the agonizing course of treatment, and her doctors' conclusion that a bone marrow transplant was her best chance. Sam was not a match. He started to explain how the national bone marrow registry worked, but Jane cut him off.

"Oscar, I get it. Sam's sister is in trouble, needs a sibling donor. Sam can't do it. There's a brother that no one has been told about, and we need to find him."

"That's about the extent of it," Oscar said.

"You have already talked with Sam's mother, and have her consent to proceed?"

"Yes, we just talked."

"Okay, I'll need to take down all the information that you have from Sam's mother – names, dates, locations, whatever you've got."

"I'm ready with all of that."

"Adoption is a matter largely regulated by the individual states. Wisconsin is among the most progressive in its law and procedures. I'll take everything you have, start digging, and see if we can find Jacob. If we do, we can make contact with him, via intermediaries, on the grounds of medical necessity. He will at that point have the option of deciding whether he wants to have any contact at all with the Mitcham family, and whether he will consent to a test as a potential bone marrow donor."

"We will be grateful for anything you can do," Oscar said.

"Who is 'we?'" Jane asked. "Does Sam know what you're doing?

"Sam doesn't know he has a brother. His mother would prefer her children not know."

"Fair enough, Oscar. I'm on it." She transcribed all the available adoption details.

Jane then put down the telephone long enough to end the connection with Oscar. She almost immediately picked it up again, and started to dial her best friend in Wisconsin.

Thirty-Four

To almost everyone outside their circle, the Matriarchs looked like a united front. Five successful women, at the top of their game, all working together to run a multi-billion dollar international law firm.

But even the most successful ruling party frays under enormous stress. The Matriarchs had to contend not only with the suspicious death of named partner Albert Rose, the murder of another named partner's primary client, but now potential criminal liability if all the rumors from Chicago turned out to be true. No one thought Armani suits would look good in prison.

At a time like this, everyone was expected to give 100 percent, and then some. Real team players would shine, like the glittering blue square-cut diamonds on each Matriarch's ring finger.

Of course, it was also a time when less than stellar performance could simply not be tolerated. Tough times didn't bode well for Matriarch Sarah. Immediately upon her return from the Chicago office, Laura summoned Sarah to her corner office.

Ironically, Sarah had the easiest Matriarch portfolio. She was in charge of marketing and public relations at a firm that basically sold itself. Most of Fishbein's partners didn't even know what Sarah did with her 35 staff, other than dodge pesky reporters, update the website, and pester them to make speeches at professional conferences. The partners firmly believed that Fishbein's success was what every new client craved. Who cared about flashy brochures and whether the logo was red or blue?

Like the other Matriarchs, Sarah was a smart woman. She started her career at Fishbein 15 years ago, left for awhile to work with an up-and-coming New Jersey law firm that never came up, and accepted Laura's offer to return. Laura Henderson figured that by rescuing Sarah from New Jersey oblivion, she would get unstinting loyalty in return. Laura had a similar deal with each of the other Matriarchs. She rescued them all, one way or another. Laura knew she could count on their intelligence and drive. Loyalty was recognized and rewarded.

"Sarah, I'm concerned that things aren't working out as well as they could, and as well as we need them to during this stressful time," Laura began, folding her hands.

Sarah had dressed for the occasion, wearing a brand new tailored suit custom-picked by Susan from Saks. "I'm afraid I don't know what you mean," she said.

"You handle the aggressive New York news media well enough, but that's mostly a matter of making sure all calls are promptly answered, and that no one really says anything a client would object to," Laura said. A basic rule of minimizing negative fallout during a crisis was to be as boring as possible, and Sarah's people hit the mark every time.

"And, to be fair, I have appreciated some of your efforts on the DeSantis case," Laura said. "Especially monitoring activities in the Chicago office, and spotlighting our need to control Sam Mitcham." It had been Sarah's idea to cut off Sam's computer access, though of course Cupcake did the dirty work. Computer control was an accepted business practice, especially at law firms.

"But the Blue Buick Incident with Oscar and Sam went way over the line," Laura said. "Poorly conceived, and badly executed."

"That was Robert's idea," Sarah said.

"It doesn't matter," Laura said. "You encouraged him. You're responsible."

"I thought it would help protect the firm," Sarah said.

"I would consider almost any option to protect this firm," Laura replied. "Encouraging the already-workaholic tendencies of over-the-hill senior partners? Yes. Homicide? No. An emphatic No!"

"Not kill them, just scare them," Sarah said, defensively. "I was just trying to help."

"That incident was bad enough, but it's not just that," Laura sighed. "Some of your other activities have not been helpful to our team at all."

"Can you give me an example?" Sarah asked.

"I can give you several examples. You've developed a nasty habit of talking about your colleagues out of turn," Laura continued. "You passed along a joke to Mindy at Connie's expense. You made a cutting remark to Connie about Carol's most recent financial report. At one point, you told Carol that one of Connie's suits was inappropriate attire for a law firm."

And all of it got back to you, Sarah thought.

"Then there was the weird thing about the allergies," Laura said. Sarah apparently had many, and spent a lot of time outside the office visiting the various specialists who cater to neurotic New Yorkers. "You're always coming back to the office with some new pill or spray or homeopathic balm, but they don't stop you from sniffling through every meeting."

"That's why you moved me?" Sarah asked.

After returning one day from her allergist du jour, Sarah sent an e-mail to Carol, passing along her allergist's speculation that perhaps mold or faulty office ventilation were to blame for her many and increasing maladies. Sarah just wanted attention, but got more than that. The other Matriarchs started to isolate her. After checking with Laura, Carol ordered Sarah's office to be boxed up and moved one floor down so that a complete health inspection could commence.

"I was fine with my old office," Sarah said. "We could've just done an office switch with a junior partner to see if that would solve the problem."

"If there was a problem with your office, we certainly wouldn't want to move anyone else in there," Laura curtly replied. "Now that it's closed up, we'll have an environmental consultant mount a full inspection."

Sarah sat quietly. She didn't have much to say, and knew the worst was still to come.

"And then there's the latest problem," Laura said. "Tell me again what happened."

"One of my staff came to me with a scheduling problem for an upcoming event. Oscar Sampson's presence had been promised for a professional seminar on 'Current Topics in Mergers and Acquisitions.' I hadn't noticed Oscar's name on the program."

"Of course he wouldn't show up," Laura said. "Oscar never shows up."

"Registrations for the conference had gone through the roof," Sarah suggested, lamely.

"Who wouldn't want to hear Oscar Sampson talk about working with the Chicago Mafia?" Laura asked.

Sarah had responded "very inappropriately" to the scheduling problem. She literally threw the conference binder across the desk at her terrified assistant, in the midst of a long string of shouted obscenities. The assistant left the building, and promptly hired her own lawyer.

Sarah's calls to Laura in Chicago, and the unwanted interruptions to Laura's interrogation of Sam, were Sarah's notification of the incident and her profound apologies. It was the last thing Laura wanted to hear. She did feel an obligation to let Sarah defend herself in person, and now that was done.

"Thank you, that will be all," Laura said. Sarah started to mumble a few words, but one look at Laura told her that this meeting was over.

As soon as Sarah left the floor, Laura was joined by the other Matriarchs – Mindy, Carol and Connie.

"I wanted to let you know that we reached a quick settlement with Sarah's assistant," Laura said. "The firm will issue a formal letter of apology. Sarah will sign it, indicating her personal regret as well."

The room was silent. The other Matriarchs knew what was coming next.

"To the larger point," Laura sighed, "I believe there's no choice but to narrow our circle. Of course, this will mean even more effort from all of us during what is already a trying time. Everyone on board?"

Mindy, Carol and Connie simply nodded. It was time to close ranks, and eliminate the weak sister. Sad, but necessary. The kind of choice that had to be made in this league.

Laura's secretary contacted Sarah's secretary, and arranged another time to meet that afternoon. Sarah thought she would have another chance to defend herself and prove her worth as a Matriarch. She cluelessly thought about making up a few quick Powerpoint slides to illustrate new business opportunities.

The next meeting was quick. A senior Human Resources official greeted Sarah in Laura's office, and told her to sit down. Laura wasn't there. She had left the building for the day, as soon as the firm's employment law experts finished their review of the necessary documents. Discretion would be expected from everyone.

By close of business, Sarah was gone. She left behind her ID card, her Fish Fone, and her brilliant blue square-cut diamond ring.

Thirty-Five

The news traveled fast: "Matriarch Sarah got sacked!"

No one sent word via computer e-mail or Fish Fones; this was the kind of news that made Fishbein employees actually talk to each other. For some, especially those in the European and Asian offices, it was the first time they had heard of Sarah. But everyone had heard about the Matriarchs, if only the story of their matching blue diamonds, and now knew that the number of ringholders was down to four.

Hundreds of Fishbein staff also heard the incredible story: Matriarch Sarah had literally thrown the book at her assistant! Everyone loved the kicker: the assistant landed well. She was said to be quite happy with a tidy settlement, letter of formal apology, and reassignment to Matriarch Connie in Legal Recruiting.

Cupcake recalibrated quickly. Sarah had been an ally, but she was gone now. *Perhaps her exit could be a chance to enhance my own stature*, he thought. *At least among the newbies.* "I've known this was coming for some time," he told Sandi, which of course was a lie, and she knew it. But it did give her an excuse to call Sam at Fishbein's Chicago office.

"Cupcake is crowing about Sarah," she said as soon as he picked up his private cell phone. Sam started to laugh. Sam had traced his computer cut-off back to Cupcake, and figured someone like Sarah had to authorize his plan.

"Couldn't happen to a nicer lady," Sam said. "Too bad they didn't take out Cupcake at the same time."

"He's not going anywhere," Sandi said. "If he can help it."

"If he's already trying to distinguish himself from Sarah with you, imagine what he's doing with the Matriarchs," Sam said.

"Do you think Sarah and Cupcake were behind the blue Buick thing?" Sandi asked.

"Who else?" Sam asked.

"There's another rumor circulating," Sandi added. "One of our secretaries has a friend in Human Resources."

"I'm all ears," Sam said.

"Apparently the other Matriarchs have been building a case against Sarah for awhile now. Her 'throwing a book' stunt was the last straw, but there were lots of others," Sandi said. "The word from HR is that they've actually got documentation of anxiety disorders, along with all the allergies. Sarah was taking lots of medication."

"So why did Laura keep her around?" Sam asked.

"That's what they're asking in HR," Sandi answered. "They're saying Laura made a simple calculation that Sarah was providing enough benefit to tolerate all of her nutsy behavior. Then, probably with a push from everything going on right now, Laura said enough was enough."

"Again, couldn't happen to a nicer lady," Sam said. "What happens to the rock?"

"That's the other hot topic of conversation. HR says Laura definitely got the ring back. The evening cleaning crew is keeping an eye out for it." Sandi laughed.

"I guess you've gotta love this stuff, and get the laughs where you can," Sam said.

"The janitors wouldn't steal it, of course," Sandi added. "They'd just make sure it was safe in the top drawer of her desk or wherever it ended up."

"So is there going to be a new Matriarch, or will Laura hold at four?" Sam asked.

Once again, Sandi had been in touch with the New York Fishbein service network on this topic. It was so much more interesting than legal grunt work. "Well, this is third-hand, but I heard that one of the secretaries talked to another secretary who is friends with Laura's assistant Toni."

"This will be information you can take to the bank. What are they saying?"

"There was no 'heir apparent' to Sarah, and the other Matriarchs have already divided up her work. Mindy will handle the public relations stuff, Connie will do the website, and Carol is doing the marketing and business development. It's as if Sarah was never here."

"So there will be no announcement of a realignment in business processes?" Sam asked.

"Not a chance. The Matriarchs have already closed ranks. They want to show Laura they can handle everything just fine without Sarah," Sandi said. "And, they probably can. No one thought she did very much."

"Didn't Sarah do a lot of plotting with Cupcake?" Sam asked. "That's what everyone in Chicago thinks. And they don't even know about the blue Buick."

"He's been seen talking separately with Mindy, Connie and Carol since the ax fell."

"Covering the bases?"

"Yep, and probably offering reassurance that whatever confidential work Sarah actually accomplished for them, he was doing all the legwork anyway."

"Oscar can't stand him," Sam said. "Especially since the Blue Buick Incident."

"And as far as the remaining Matriarchs are concerned, that's perfect," Sandi said. "There's no question of loyalty in their power struggle with Oscar Sampson."

"Well," Sam said, "I guess it's good to know we picked the right side."

Thirty-Six

Sam was as surreptitiously entertained as anyone by Sarah's departure. And he was as concerned as anyone by the implications of the DeSantis case. But mostly, if he had to name what was really keeping him up at night, he was heartsick at the prospects for his sister Theresa. For someone trained in sizing up situations as Sam had been in law school, it just didn't look good for her.

Here's the hard, cold calculation that he couldn't shake: *Theresa was about to lose the lottery, AGAIN!*

Number one: aggressive breast cancer. Number two: acute myeloid leukemia, as the oncologist said, "secondary to breast cancer." And now, number three: no suitable match for a bone marrow transplant.

Sam trusted Sandi now, so he brought it up as soon as she finished telling him the "Sarah Go Boom" update. She listened intently, and then started asking questions like the not-so-objective lawyer she had become.

"How are you calculating her odds?" was her first question.

"Ten thousand is the first relevant statistic," Sam said, reflecting the amount of time he had been surfing the Web for answers. "That's the number of people who are diagnosed each year with diseases whose best hope is a bone-marrow transplant.

Leukemia, sickle cell anemia, all of that."

"Keep going," she said. Sandi knew how Sam's brain was working. She just wanted to catch up.

"About 30 percent of those needing transplants get a match from a family member," Sam said. "A sibling has a 25 percent chance of being a match. Parents have a five percent match. Theresa's mother and her brother do not match."

"Then there's the registry," Sandi said.

"Right, the registry," Sam sighed. "The other 70 percent look to the registry, which has millions of people on it from all over the world. The likelihood of finding a match on the registry actually sounds pretty good, something from 60 to 90 percent, depending on ethnicity. White people make up three-quarters of the registry, African-Americans and Hispanics about ten percent each."

"That does sound pretty good. Your sister is a white woman."

"Right, but a few of her so-called 'markers' are pretty unique. She's allergic to a lot of things."

"Well, I understand that one," Sandi said. "I've been fighting lots of allergies since I was a little girl – allergic to penicillin, allergic to antibiotics…"

"Theresa has all that and more."

"So they've already searched the registry, and there's no one?"

"No one yet, no."

Sam was tired of thinking about this, and was out of ideas. Sandi was just getting started.

"How about if we try getting more people added to the registry, so that there would be more possible matches?"

"Mom and I would be willing to try anything."

"No, I'm thinking of a practical way to add a significant chunk of white people in their '20s to the registry." She paused for a second, and for once Sam was the one who needed to catch up … with her.

"Law students. New associates at law firms like Fishbein," she said.

"How?"

"E-mail alerts. Law student websites and blogs. Electronic alumni billboards at first-tier schools like yours, and the lesser schools like mine," she said, starting to laugh at the scope of her brilliant idea.

"This is good," Sam said, instantly getting it.

"I'm sure Matriarch Connie in Legal Recruiting would love something positive to talk about, instead of having to dodge questions about DeSantis and whether it means the end of the world as we know it."

"This is really good," Sam said, almost able to hear the gears turning in Sandi's head, even though he was in Chicago, and she in New York.

"I'm talking while I'm thinking ... not usually the best practice for a first-year associate," Sandi said.

"Oh, but here's a glitch," Sam said.

"What?"

"Good news is that the test is easy ... just a cheek swab. Bad news is that reading the test is expensive. About a hundred bucks a pop. The cost factor is why lots of public appeals for donors don't fly."

"So we would need funding," Sandi said.

"Yeah, potentially a significant chunk of it. Let's say we were able to recruit 5,000 law students and associates to get tested. That would cost 500 grand."

"But even if we didn't find a match for your sister, that would still be 5,000 new healthy donors in the registry, who could help someone else."

"Yes, that's all true."

"Why don't you talk to Oscar, and I'll talk to Connie," Sandi said, providing the next strategic action steps.

Sam got through to Oscar before Sandi was able to talk with Connie. For Oscar Sampson, who knew it was too soon to tell whether Jacob could be located, let alone consent to a test or end up a match, the additional opportunity presented by Sam and Sandi was truly a no-brainer.

"If the firm turns this down," he said to Sam, "I'll pay for it myself."

Thirty-Seven

Fishbein, Schindler, Rose and Sampson did not turn it down. "This is brilliant," Laura said to Robert. "Take it out of the pro bono budget."

Cupcake was eager to implement Matriarch Connie's new initiative. Connie pitched it as a way to reassure all her doubting recruits that Fishbein actually had a heart, despite the sudden departure of Albert Rose and that nasty DeSantis case in Chicago. Laura thought it was even bigger than that.

Sam set up a three-way conference call with his Mom and Sandi to review the plan – Sandi from New York, Sam from Chicago, and his Mom in Milwaukee.

"Hi, Mrs. Mitcham," Sandi said to start the call.

"Hello," Barbara Mitcham replied. "I'm glad to hear that Sam has made a good friend at the law firm." Sam's Mom had been wondering if Sandi was more than a friend. Her name had been coming up a lot lately in the other telephone conversations between Sam and his Mom.

"Sandi has come up with a terrific idea," Sam said. "And what's even better, she's getting the Big Fish to pay for it."

"Does Oscar know you call his firm the Big Fish?" Sam's Mom asked.

"Oscar's a sharp guy," Sam said. "I don't think he misses much."

"He never did," Barbara Mitcham said. "So, Sandi, tell me about your plan."

Sandi reviewed the broad outlines, much in the way a lawyer would detail a legal strategy for a new client. Of course, in this case the client was a very sick woman who was fighting to stay alive.

"This is amazing," Barbara Mitcham said.

"And it's going to work," Sam said. "Especially since Sandi convinced the Matriarchs to pay for it."

"We have up to $500,000 to spend on donor testing," Sandi said. "At minimum, we'll add 5,000 potential donors to the registry. One or more of them could be Theresa's match."

Most conference call presentations of legal strategy don't end with the participants starting to cry. This one did. Sam was glad they were on the phone in different cities, so his Mom and Sandi couldn't see that he was crying too.

Barbara Mitcham promised to share this news with Theresa as soon as she could. "She's having a rough time of it right now, but this will definitely brighten her spirits," she said.

For her part, Sam's Mom felt a thrill she could only share with her friend Oscar – the potential for both of her sons to be involved in a cure for their sister. He would urge the caution expected of a senior lawyer, but could barely contain his glee.

"Law Students Unite to Save Leukemia Victim" took off quickly. The e-mails and blog posts and news stories pretty much wrote themselves. Barbara Mitcham, Sandi and Sam provided compelling interviews, and encouraged the growing conversations on Facebook, YouTube, Flickr, and the other social media sites. Theresa couldn't be photographed, so everyone just passed along her high school graduation picture. Who wouldn't want to help?

The public relations folks treated Matriarch Connie's initiative as the blessing it was. They knew it would completely switch Fishbein's PR liability away from the DeSantis case. Even the normally bitchy legal and business media ran with it. No one thought to mention that Matriarch Sarah, who used to run the PR operation, was no longer around. The lingering questions about Albert Rose were completely buried by the buzz surrounding the new campaign.

The pitch was simple: "We're asking students to put down their law books for five minutes, and help us."

Helping was easy: "Send us your name and address. We'll get the testing kit mailed to you. Swab your cheek, and send it back."

"Sponsored by Fishbein, Schindler, Rose and Sampson."

Thirty-Eight

New York City's Bryant Park is the busiest public space in the country – its one city block includes the main branch of the public library, two restaurants, a fountain, a carousel, statues of forgotten celebrities, a great lawn which hosts picnickers in summer and skaters in winter, and the constant foot traffic of thousands of pedestrians.

The subway station underneath Bryant Park is known as the noisiest among all the stations serving New York's five boroughs of Manhattan, Brooklyn, Staten Island, Queens, and the Bronx.

With its rush of activity and anonymity, Bryant Park seemed the perfect place for Jane Chapnick to meet Jacob.

Having spent so many years in child and family law, it wasn't surprising to Jane that Jacob ended up not in the Midwest, but in New York City. *People bounce around a lot,* she thought.

Jane and her friends had been very careful contacting Jacob. By suggesting a meeting in Bryant Park, she meant to reassure him that she just wanted to talk. He did not risk an ambush.

They met at the subway stop on the southwest corner of Bryant Park, at the intersection of 42nd Street and 6th Avenue. Jane arrived 15 minutes ahead of their scheduled time, and wore her red hat so Jacob could easily identify her.

She could tell right away he was Sam's brother. A bit older, but the same jaw line, same expressive eyes, even the same walk.

Jacob had already picked up the *Daily News*, and read the story titled "Law Students Unite to Save Leukemia Victim." The story included Theresa's high school graduation picture. He had never met her, but saw something familiar in her eyes.

"Hi!" Jane said, offering her hand. "Thanks for coming in." She could see the *Daily News* in his left hand. "This must be very weird for you."

"I'm okay, thanks," was the first thing Jacob said.

"It's a lovely day," Jane said, "How about a little walk in the park?"

"Sure."

They started walking around the perimeter of the lawn, joining the flow of the thousands of people who moved through this space every hour.

"How's she doing?" Jacob asked.

"Who?"

"Theresa Mitcham," Jacob said, pointing to her high school picture in the newspaper.

"Well, not so great right now."

This was not going the way Jane Chapnick expected. She thought they would talk for awhile about Jacob's life, his history and what he was doing now. But Jacob, just minutes after meeting Jane at one of the busiest places on the planet, wanted to cut to the chase. If Oscar Sampson had been watching, he would've said, "Well, he is Barbara and Larry's son."

"A bone marrow transplant is her best shot, right?" Jacob asked.

Jane Chapnick dropped her agenda. Jacob was running this meeting.

"It's probably her only shot," she said.

"And what are the chances I'd be a match?"

"A sibling has the best chance, because you have the same

parents and genetic material. But the other biological sibling didn't match." Jane regretted this choice of words as soon as it came out of her mouth. Too clinical. She was about to correct herself when Jacob again cut to the chase.

"Yeah, the story said that Sam isn't a match."

"Right," she said, looking into his eyes. The same steely determination she often saw in Sam.

"So, if I get tested, and if I'm a match, they have to punch big needles into my back to remove the bone marrow, right?" he asked. Jacob had been reading, but the book he found was old.

"No, but that's how it used to be," she said. "In most cases, they just give you a medication that forces the marrow from your bones into your bloodstream. They hook you up to a machine, and the extraction process works a lot like a blood donation."

Jacob was silent, taking in this information.

Jane looked away from him for a moment, her gaze shifting to all the other people in the park.

"I would do it either way," Jacob said. "Whatever she needs."

"Yeah," Jane said, completely dropping the careful guise of a lawyer. "I knew you would."

An open bench appeared on their path. Jacob motioned for Jane to sit down, and she followed his lead. They were both lost in their own thoughts for awhile, while watching the continuing parade of pedestrians bustling through the park.

"This is a lot to take in all at once," Jacob finally said.

"I know it is."

"I knew I was adopted, but I didn't know about Sam or Theresa."

"They don't know anything about you."

"I was told the adoption records were sealed."

"They are, but we're able to make contact in case of a medical emergency, like this one."

"You said Sam and Theresa don't know about me. What about

my biological parents?" Jacob asked, already knowing the first part of the answer.

"Your biological father passed away five years ago. Your biological mother lives in Milwaukee, and she authorized us to make contact."

"Does she want to meet me?" Jacob asked, swallowing hard.

"I don't know, but I'm sure she would. Up until a week ago, she thought the records were completely sealed. That's the way it was explained when you were born, and they just lived with it that way."

"So she doesn't know anything about my life."

"No. And she doesn't know you live here in New York. It can stay that way if you want."

Jacob didn't have the legal training of his little brother, but he knew enough to take this potentially overwhelming situation one step at a time.

"Okay," he said, "let's worry about first things first. How do I get tested?"

"That part is pretty easy," Jane said, pulling out a form that said, "Donor Registration and Consent for HLA Typing." She also had a long envelope with two sealed cotton swabs, with a card that said, "How to Use Your Buccal Swab Kit."

"It's just Q-Tips," Jacob said.

"And a self-addressed stamped envelope to send it all in."

Jane handed the packet to Jacob, and again followed his lead as he stood up. This was more than enough information for their first meeting.

"I'll get this in the mail today," he said, shaking Jane's hand before heading back to the world's noisiest subway station.

Jacob was probably the most important potential donor to complete a test that day, but he wasn't the only one. Sandi swabbed her own sample test first, and then coordinated the collection of the tests of several hundred partners, associates and support staff of Fishbein, Schindler, Rose and Sampson –

including all four remaining Matriarchs.

Laura was first in line. Before anyone else, and before the publicity cameras showed up.

Thirty-Nine

Good lawyers always go into meetings prepared. They think through, in advance, what might be discussed, and what questions can be anticipated. They have their own agenda of what they'd like to accomplish, with the understanding that since they're counsel and not client, the best they may be able to do is shape the outcome – not control it. If they can bill premium rates for their preparation time, so much the better. A good lawyer prepares whether he's getting paid or not.

As Sam sped along on I-94 from Chicago to Milwaukee, he was rehearsing what would probably happen in his next meeting. Trouble was, when the meeting was with his sister and his mother, the odds of shaping the outcome were pretty slim. They were family, not clients. *Real Matriarchs*, he thought to himself.

Sam was truly heartened by all the attention around the "Law Students Unite to Save Leukemia Victim" story, especially the way Sandi was running with it. He knew the national bone marrow donor registry was probably going to get thousands of new listings. A lot of people were learning about how they could directly impact someone else's life, and even save the life of someone they'd probably never meet.

He intended to convey a sense of hope at this next meeting, because there was every reason to hope. *There always is*, he thought.

The part he kept trying to swallow was the odds that a match would actually be found in time for Theresa. He didn't match, and he was her blood brother. His odds would be as good as anyone, at about 25 percent. It went down from there. The "needle in a haystack" line kept popping into his head, and whenever it did he tuned to a new station on the rental car's satellite radio.

I'm going into this meeting positive and upbeat, he thought. He would be ready with stories of Fishbein and the DeSantis case and the murder investigation as back-up. In any other meeting, that would be more than enough. *But this is my sister, and my sister is probably going to die soon.* That was just the cold hard fact. She didn't have much time, and with all her allergies and physical vulnerabilities, the doctors needed a lot of stars to line up for a viable match.

It was a Sunday, so there wasn't much traffic. Sam was able to zoom past Milwaukee's downtown and out towards the suburban medical center housing the bone marrow transplant unit. There was plenty of parking in the hospital garage, and no one waiting for the elevators. Once in the lobby, Sam barely took notice of a line of wheelchairs, waiting for other patients on other days.

Sam knew the ritual of entering the BMT unit. He smiled at the receptionist, threw his coat over one of the hooks in the hallway, and went to the special sink to wash his hands. There was a stack of the scratchy surgical masks next to the sink.

The last few years' history surged into his brain, and he almost said out loud his mantra for this meeting: *Just suck it up.*

He expected to see both mother and sister in the room; but it was just Theresa this time. Her eyes were closed, but sprang to life as soon as her baby brother walked in the room.

"Hey, beautiful," Sam said.

"Hey, bullshitter," Theresa replied. She managed a slight smile, but he could immediately feel how much she was hurting. He remembered some of the lines he rehearsed on the way up from Chicago.

"Bet you thought that high school graduation picture was safe inside the old yearbook," he said

"Well, at least I had hair then," she said, with a shrug.

"We had to give them something. Put a face on the story, as the PR folks say."

"It's the best face I've got these days."

"Point is, it's working. We think a couple thousand people are signing up for the registry."

"Well, that is pretty impressive. Maybe there's a match for me in there somewhere."

"I bet there is," Sam said.

"What does Mom always say? Your mouth to God's ear?"

"I'm fine with the prospect of divine intervention," Sam said, and meant it.

They were quiet for awhile. Behind the mask, Sam ran through a few of the stories he had prepared for this meeting. He let them go. This was his sister, and he could sense that she wasn't in the mood, or didn't have the energy, for tales of life at Fishbein, Schindler, Rose and Sampson.

"How's Sandi?" Theresa finally asked.

"She's actually kind of amazing," Sam said. "She did all the work on this law student thing. She was first to get tested, and even got the Matriarchs in line behind her. I think she may have even snared Cupcake into getting swabbed."

"That's the guy who used to be called Robert, right?" Theresa asked.

"Yeah, but turns out he'd do anything to get ahead at the firm," Sam said. "Cupcake is actually about the nicest thing Sandi and I could call him."

"Just my luck if a dick like that ended up being a match," she said. Sick people, like old people, stop caring about the propriety of what they say. As for Cupcake, Sam completely agreed with

Theresa's assessment, but would roll out a red carpet if he actually was a match.

"Tell me more about Sandi," Theresa said.

"She's my buddy at Fishbein. I tell her everything I know, and I think she does the same. I listen to her stuff, and she listens to mine. I think we 'get' each other."

"Do I smell romance in the air?" Theresa asked.

"Well, I'm in the Midwest, and she's in New York, so nothing yet," Sam said. "But she's starting to feel like family."

"That's what I was thinking, too," Theresa said.

The other member of the Mitcham family entered the room, holding a mask over her mouth but not her nose.

"Hey, put that on all the way," Theresa told her mother.

Sam could see that his mother's eyes were wet. She'd been crying. *God knows there's plenty of reason to cry,* he thought.

But Sam couldn't quite figure out the furrows on his Mom's brow. She mumbled through some small talk with her children, but her mind seemed to be somewhere else. Sam could see she was carrying a cell phone in her hand, and wondered if she had been talking to someone.

Barbara Mitcham had just taken a call from Oscar Sampson.

"I've only got a minute, but wanted to share some good news," he said.

"What?" she asked, in the shorthand of old friends.

"Jacob has been located, and agreed to be tested as a possible match for Theresa," Oscar said.

"Does he want to meet me, Sam and Theresa?" Barbara asked.

"One thing at a time, my dear," Oscar said, like the good counsel he was. "If there's a way to bring you together, you know I'll make it happen."

Forty

Sandi hadn't been to the Columbia campus since she applied to its law school four years earlier. She hadn't been accepted then, but was being welcomed with open arms now.

Sam had reminded her not to wear high heels, since the cobblestone walk between the subway stop at 116th Street and the Law School a block away was notorious for ruining women's shoes. No mortar between the cobblestones. Sandi knew it wouldn't be a problem, since her current Matriarch-approved wardrobe included only sensible flats.

Columbia Law School's main building was known affectionately as the "Toaster," not because of the heat generated inside, but simply because the faculty lounge protruding from the side of the metallic modernist box really gave the appearance from the outside of the kitchen appliance.

"You must be Sandi," Jane Chapnick said, extending her hand as Sandi entered the Toaster. Jane was accompanied by several earnest-looking law students.

"Hi. Sam has told me a lot about you," Sandi said. "You were his favorite professor."

Jane Chapnick smiled, knowing her current students were hearing the praise.

"But I still lost him to the Big Fish," Jane said, with a nod towards her current Child Advocacy Clinic students. Maybe she would be luckier with them.

"I have 50 of the donor swab kits for you, just as you asked," Sandi said.

"I can take those," one of the students said. This lawyer-in-training was dressed in jeans and a cool shirt. Sandi remembered when her student wardrobe would have fit right in. Not so much anymore. Now she looked like a conservative corporate lawyer.

"Thank you for everything you guys have already done to spread the word," Sandi said.

"We're happy to do it," said the student. "But for all the Luddites who don't spend every waking moment on Facebook, we'll get these directly into their hands."

"The personal touch always helps," said Professor Chapnick.

"Good to meet you," the lawyer-in-training said. "We've got to head back to class."

"Thanks again," Sandi said, as the students darted into the bowels of the Toaster.

"Have you got a few minutes to chat?" Jane asked.

"Sure," Sandi replied. "They won't miss me at Fishbein for a little while."

Jane Chapnick led Sandi across the street to the thin five-story building which housed all of Columbia Law School's clinical programs. Jane's office was on the top floor, with a view of Harlem to the north.

"How is Sam holding up?" Jane asked, as soon as Sandi had settled into a chair. Jane knew the odds for success with the "Law Students Unite to Save Leukemia Victim" campaign were about to increase, but that news could not come from her.

"I don't think either of us expected our first year of corporate law to turn out the way it has," Sandi said. "You can read most of it on the law student blogs."

"I've been keeping up," Jane said. "I also talk with Oscar Sampson once in awhile."

"Talk about a man with his hands full," Sandi said.

"Last founding partner standing, murdered client, and the Matriarchs," Jane said. "Quite a handful, indeed."

"You know about the Matriarchs?" Sandi asked.

"I know all about them," Jane replied. "I probably could have been one of them."

"Didn't Matriarch Connie come from Columbia Law?" asked Sandi.

"Yes, she did," Jane said. "But Laura recruited Mindy and Carol first,"

"You know more than I do," Sandi said.

"Let me fill in the blanks for you," Jane Chapnick said, like the professor she was. "For decades, Oscar Sampson and Laura Henderson recognized their mutual importance to the growing multi-national legal powerhouse known as Fishbein, Schindler, Rose and Sampson. Oscar's name was on the door of 22 offices around the world. Laura kept the lights on, and put the fires out."

"That's quite an opening statement, professor," Sandi said.

"Well, I do have a tendency to go on," Jane said. "But this is a story that doesn't need much embellishment."

"Please, do go on," Sandi said.

"They'd certainly had their differences over the years," Professor Chapnick said. "Oscar wasn't an early advocate of ceding so much operational power to Laura, but he accepted Morris Fishbein's argument that the arrangement left him free to practice his kind of law."

Sandi looked at Jane, wondering if Fishbein's kind of law was really the kind of law she wanted to be associated with.

"In an early memorable meeting, Fishbein laid it on the line: 'Laura is perfect for us,' he said. 'She doesn't have a life. She has this firm. We couldn't ask for anything better.' Messrs. Schindler, Rose and Sampson found themselves nodding in agreement."

Sandi wasn't nodding.

"Under Laura, the Big Fish became the envy of corporate law, and the model many others tried unsuccessfully to copy," the professor continued. "The pretenders looked at the flat business model, with all the top people at the director level – no vice presidents running around, like the corporate clients. They looked at Fishbein's expansion plan, bringing in new practices just a little in advance of when individual markets demanded it. They looked at Fishbein's staff support model, with secretaries all paid based on their years of service to the firm, not whether they supported star partners. They looked at the firm's early and enthusiastic support of pro bono programs, always ensuring the recruitment of the most dedicated and enthusiastic legal talent from law schools – even though most corporate law is dreary legal grunt work."

"Yeah, I've become familiar with the grunt work part," Sandi said.

"But what none of the pretenders ever got, though it was in plain view, was Laura's development and nurturing of the Matriarchs. Specifically, recruiting powerful women to individually manage significant chunks of the business, while at the same time working as an elite sisterhood," Jane said. "It was brilliant."

"It *was* brilliant," Sandi agreed.

"Morris Fishbein trained Laura Henderson himself, tested her under extreme circumstances, and treated her as the protégé she was. He planted the idea of a matriarchy with her, and specifically funded the wearable symbol of their influence and leadership – the huge, blue, square-cut diamond rings. Only a Matriarch could wear the rock, and if she left – as was the unfortunate case with Sarah – the big diamond stayed at the Big Fish."

"You've already heard about Sarah?" Sandi asked. "That just happened."

Professor Chapnick was just getting warmed up, and ignored Sandi's question. Of course she knew about Sarah.

"With Morris Fishbein's encouragement, Laura devoured

every management and business psychology textbook she could find," Jane said. "She attended numerous evening and weekend courses at New York's leading business schools, picking up an MBA in the process. Fishbein paid every bill, and instituted a tuition reimbursement policy for other employees, a first among corporate law firms. Best money he ever spent."

"The irony of encouraging this internal structure while developing ruthless legal tactics including the 'hostile takeover' and the 'poison pill' was not lost on the firm's founding partners, was it?" Sandi asked.

This question was worthy of comment by the professor. "The surprising thing was that other firms didn't copy Fishbein's matriarchal model. They just copied the little, insignificant stuff, which suited Morris Fishbein and his partners just fine. They reworked the practice of corporate law while all the established firms just watched and wondered."

"Amazing," Sandi said.

"Laura thought the Fishbein Matriarchs should include six women, since that was the number reinforced as the optimal business unit through her MBA training," Professor Chapnick said. "The magical number six for Fishbein was reinforced when one of Morris Fishbein's early clients inquired about the possibility of a trade in lieu of case payment for a mounting legal bill."

"Free diamonds," Sandi said.

"Well, not exactly free," Jane said. "The client had six identical, and rare, square-cut blue diamonds. They had come from one of the client's operations in South Africa. Would they compensate for two years' worth of unpaid Fishbein bills? Morris happily cut the deal, and presented the treasure to his brilliant protégé the next day. The Matriarchs were born."

"And then the recruiting began?" Sandi asked.

"Laura had learned through her MBA training that there is no better guarantee of loyalty than rescue – simply put, if you save someone, they'll watch your back," Jane said. "She began to look for other women she could rescue, and bring into the fold. There was no rush, since the firm was being adequately managed by standard-issue business practices and personnel. She had the luxury of time to find the right women."

"Matriarch Mindy was first," Sandi said.

"Laura was probably put off at the idea of hiring someone named 'Mindy.' Sounded too Southern California, or something," Jane said. "Mindy was an underappreciated legal administrator Laura met at one of her night classes. Like Laura, Mindy was an ambitious woman looking for a better life. Unlike Laura, Mindy didn't have a mentor like Morris Fishbein. What she did have, at her white shoe law firm, was more than a few partners who didn't like the idea of a strong, smart woman supervising their caseloads."

"I can just imagine how it went," Sandi said. "One evening, Mindy showed up at night class with red eyes. Laura could see she'd been crying, but in spite of whatever happened, was determined to show up for class. Laura took Mindy out for dinner after class that evening, and heard the story. Mindy had been told that afternoon that her firm no longer required her services."

"Probably not too far off," the professor said.

Mindy would never forget that Laura held her hand that night, and told her that no matter what anyone else said, Laura knew talent when she saw it. And Laura followed through, facilitating an interview with Morris Fishbein two days later, and a job offer by the end of the week.

Mindy had been rescued, and gratefully joined Fishbein, Schindler, Rose and Sampson. She was tireless as Laura's first recruit, and made an early mark at her new firm by helping to bring over several clients from her old firm.

About a month into her new job, Mindy complimented Laura on her beautiful blue square-cut diamond ring. Laura took Mindy into her office, explained the Matriarch philosophy, and presented Mindy with the second diamond.

"Once again, Laura saw Mindy's reddened eyes, but this time it was from tears of joy," Sandi said, completely picking up Jane Chapnick's professorial narrative. "They went to the jeweler together to have Mindy's diamond set into a ring just like Laura's."

Mindy was Laura's first Matriarch, and so was always a little more special than the other women they recruited. Mindy got the really delicate assignments, because Laura trusted her and knew Mindy could handle them.

Professor Chapnick continued with the story: "Mindy knew Carol from one of the banks she had done business with before Fishbein. She had a similar history – a smart woman who became senior in her field before business culture shifted to accept women in senior ranks. Carol was appreciated by the league of first vice presidents at her bank, but they let her know in a thousand ways that she'd never be permitted to join them."

"They would always be happy, however, to take credit for her hard work," Sandi said.

"Carol's pattern at the bank followed Mindy's pattern at the white shoe law firm. She got to the position of either too much knowledge or too much power. One too many of her male colleagues felt threatened. They ganged up on her, concocted some legally viable excuse, and showed her the door," Jane said.

"Mindy was waiting, with an introduction to Laura," Sandi said.

"The three women recognized kindred spirits over dinner, and Carol had an offer by the end of the week from Fishbein, Schindler, Rose and Sampson. Carol left her bank job with her pride intact, an emotional connection to the Matriarchs, and her old bank colleagues wondering what the hell happened," Jane said.

At Fishbein, Carol had a significant investment portfolio to manage, and an open invitation to implement every good idea she'd ever had. Within a month, much to her delight, she also had her very own blue, square-cut diamond ring. She became the Matriarch who watched the money.

"Your former colleague Connie was next?" Sandi asked.

"Connie was the director of the career services office at Columbia," Jane said. "It was her job to feed students into white shoe law firms. She worked hard, but was always assured of traditional success. With a 99 percent placement rate, every student who wanted a job got one – usually their first choice among several attractive offers."

"Did Connie get bored here?" Sandi asked, remembering that her own experience was one of trying and failing to get in Columbia Law's door.

"Connie's face was pressed against a glass ceiling," Jane said. "She was already an assistant dean at the law school, so there was nowhere else to go. Also, even though she was directly connected to the moneyed and influential law firms, as an administrator she was definitely a second-class citizen. The academic world is a caste system that puts faculty at the top of the pile."

"Lawyers like to rank things, don't they?" Sandi asked. Jane nodded affirmatively.

"Connie met Carol and Mindy while on a recruiting visit to Fishbein. Though most law firms weren't aware of the emerging Matriarchs, Connie could sense it. She was ready to switch leagues, and made the bold suggestion that Fishbein elevate its legal recruiting operation to a cabinet-level post. If it did, she would be interested," Jane said.

"Carol and Mindy were interested too," Sandi said.

"Yes, and made the case to Laura that law schools meant future success to Fishbein," the professor said. "Specifically, the firm could target the growing population of female law students, like you, with programs designed specifically for them. Fishbein could lead New York firms now responding more and more to the feminist movement. Their piece of it would be decidedly from within the established system, but that was the whole point – change from the inside."

"So, just as Fishbein was scooping up work that white shoe firms didn't want to do, Fishbein could recruit young women who other firms would employ, but wouldn't nurture," Sandi said. "And, it would be good business."

"Most of Connie's Columbia Law School colleagues figured she was going to Fishbein for the money, and that was partly true," Jane said. "Her starting salary would be 50 percent higher than what she was earning after years in academia."

What Connie didn't mention was the unique leadership group she had pitched her way into, and how excited she felt by their resulting invitation. The blue square-cut diamond ring came a month later, and just seemed to confirm her instinct that this was the right move.

"Sarah came last – and didn't last," Sandi said.

Laura regarded the rescue of Sarah as a mistake, and the less said the better. On that, the Matriarchs never argued. Jane Chapnick had no other lesson to add.

Laura's initial plan, supported by her mentor Morris Fishbein, was a firm run by six Matriarchs. The current count was four, and holding. Future growth would take a back seat, for now, to solving the problems created by the one remaining founding partner – Oscar Sampson.

Forty-One

Law firm partners in Oscar Sampson's league know how to juggle.

Along with a significant personal caseload, and the responsibility to grow existing clients and find new ones, the managing partners of major corporate law firms are effectively running billion-dollar businesses.

Morris Fishbein, David Schindler, Albert Rose, and Oscar Sampson ceded major operational responsibility to the Matriarchs, but they never forgot whose names were on the door. Over the years, Laura proved herself in countless ways over an immense variety of situations. Fishbein led the pack in every new development of corporate law – if you wanted the guys with the best track record, the list started and ended with the Big Fish. The list of who could run the back office started and ended with Laura Henderson.

But now Fishbein, Schindler, and Rose were gone. Oscar Sampson was 63 years old. His major contribution to the growth of the firm, the care and feeding of DeSantis Industries, was in the intensive care unit. The principal client was dead. Peter DeSantis' money trail, if it included money laundering, could bring down the firm.

But it's often said that in every crisis lies an opportunity.

Laura knew that the stakes were high, but that the successful handling of this matter could cement the Matriarchs' control of the firm. Oscar Sampson knew it too. This wasn't exactly how he envisioned his life at 63 turning out, but he still had a few cards to play. If he could also juggle a few favors for his friend Barbara Mitcham and her wiseass son, so much the better.

Oscar and Laura didn't deal with each other much in person, and hadn't for years. In fact, they hadn't been in the same room since Laura introduced Sam to Oscar. Oscar had done his best to appear disheartened that time, even though he was eager to bring Sam into his camp. Laura had since figured out that one, and knew the stakes were now too high for any more missteps. Especially after the embarrassing Blue Buick Incident.

Laura had the administrative machinery of a major law firm at her disposal. She would take pains to ensure that her directives could not be immediately traced to her.

Laura's latest idea would need to be vetted before it could be implemented. For this delicate task, she went to Mindy, her first recruit. Laura proposed a private lunch. For everyone on Fishbein's Client Conference Floor, it was a relatively routine request: lunch for two in the small corner conference room. Attendees would be Laura and Mindy. The room was prepared an hour in advance, and the in-house caterer made a couple of salads – because that's what the two Matriarchs always ate.

Because she was a woman who always thought through her next couple of steps, Laura had her assistant Toni call Cupcake, with a request that he be available during the lunch hour. He wasn't invited to lunch; he was asked to "be available." Cupcake felt there was potential fallout from his role in executing the Blue Buick Incident, but also smelled potential opportunity. *Oscar is a bigger problem than I am,* he thought, *and I can help them deal with him.* He started staring at his phone 15 minutes in advance of the scheduled meeting, waiting for his chance.

Laura and Mindy arrived at the Client Conference Floor separately. Mindy knew something momentous was on tap, and was dutifully thrilled to once again be taken into Laura's strictest confidence. These two women had navigated so many storms before, and their track record together was almost perfect.

They sat together for a short time, sharing small talk about nothing, while the waiter brought in their salads. They continued chatting while they ate, and began intense discussion after the door closed.

A short time later, Mindy called Cupcake's line. It was all he could do to not run up the stairs to their meeting. He forced himself to take the elevator, so he could appear composed. The Matriarchs had no doubt he would carry whatever water they had in mind. Especially since Sarah was the one axed after the Blue Buick Incident, not him. Of course, it didn't help that Sarah threw a book at a Fishbein assistant.

"Robert," Mindy began, "We have an important matter to discuss, and of course this is highly sensitive." Laura didn't say a word; she didn't have to.

"How can I help?" he asked.

"We need you to conduct a confidential inquiry for us," Mindy said.

Robert began nodding. *Whatever they want.*

"How are your relationships with our junior litigation partners?" Mindy asked. Mindy knew those partners pretty well herself, not to mention the finer details of their individual caseloads, billable quarter-hours, and expense requisitions.

Cupcake was taken aback for a moment. What would Mindy and Laura want from the firm's courtroom sharks that they couldn't ask for themselves? But he was a smart man, and capable of thinking on his feet.

"I can certainly discern the answers to sensitive questions without prompting idle office gossip, if that's what you mean," he said.

That was exactly what they meant.

"We're troubled by the implications of the DeSantis case,"

Mindy said.

"Do you mean the potential criminal liability connected to the allegations that Peter DeSantis was involved in money laundering, perhaps with the knowledge or assistance of our remaining founding partner?"

That was exactly what they meant.

"Based on what we know about the client's history, and current situation, could you produce a realistic assessment for us of the firm's criminal liability under a variety of scenarios?" Mindy asked.

"Of course I can," he replied. "A good deal of that assessment is already available, and could quickly be pieced together."

"Thank you," Mindy said, and looked to Laura.

"Robert, we know there's a nightmare scenario, in which the firm is directly threatened and people go to jail," Laura said.

"I will do my best to completely map out that risk."

"We want you to go beyond that," Laura said. This time, Robert didn't know where she was going.

"Along with mapping out the scenarios, we want an assessment of cutting the firm's losses," she said. "By that I mean whether we should proactively contact the appropriate law enforcement authorities, and tell them what we know."

Robert looked blankly at the two Matriarchs. This kind of thinking is what got them where they were. "Find out if it's time for us to go the FBI," Laura said.

Forty-Two

Laura wasn't the only one thinking ahead, and employing surrogates. Laura had the Matriarchs and Cupcake; Oscar Sampson had Sam Mitcham. And, much as Laura had just upped the ante with her people, Oscar was about to do the same with his.

Good lawyers have a bit of actor in them. They know the value of a good entrance.

Oscar chose the BMT unit in Milwaukee. Getting there was easy enough. With one phone call, Oscar was able to arrange a quick one-way shuttle flight and limo to the hospital. He could count on Sam to chauffeur the return trip.

When Oscar arrived, Theresa was asleep in her room. Sam and his Mom were sitting by themselves in the waiting room. Oscar strolled in, wearing a sharp tailored suit, his typical uniform. Sam was wearing a baseball cap and sweats. Barbara Mitcham was a little more turned out, but hadn't been paying much attention to appearances.

"I would've brought flowers, but I don't think they're allowed here," Oscar said, shaking Sam's startled hand and offering Barbara a quick hug. "How's our patient?"

Barbara's last contact with Oscar was a cell phone conversation about Jacob: he had been contacted, he would be tested, she could hope for a meeting later. *Was Oscar bringing word of a successful match?* she wondered.

"She's hanging in there," Sam said. What he meant was: *she's hanging by a thread.*

"We haven't heard anything about a match, yet," Barbara said, meaning to start a sentence that Oscar could complete with good news. He didn't. Oscar didn't know Jacob's test results, and had a different agenda for this meeting. All three were standing. It didn't occur to anyone to sit down.

"I'm so heartened that she's getting the best possible care," Oscar said, turning to Barbara Mitcham. "I'm keeping my fingers crossed that we'll find a match."

Barbara looked down. She understood. Nothing yet.

"Meantime, the world of work intrudes once again, and we must return to Chicago. Sam, can I hitch a ride with you?"

Sam knew in an instant that his family time was over. As Oscar had appeared in person to remind him, he had pressing responsibilities to his employer. "You go," his Mom said, "I'll talk to you later. You too, Mr. Sampson." She cast a hopeful look in Oscar's direction.

The drive from Milwaukee's suburbs to Chicago would take about an hour and a half, probably less at the speed Sam usually traveled. Sam's initial thought was to take it slow, until Oscar lit up a cigarette in the front seat of the rental car. Sam was reminded of Oscar's three-martini-lunch history, and felt free to drive fast.

"Things are heating up," Oscar began, rolling down his window so he could flick away the dangling ash from his cigarette. Oscar came of age when everyone smoked, and remained loyal to the Kent brand. He smoked less now, almost never in public spaces. But in the car with his protégé, it was a signal of deepening trust.

"What are the Matriarchs up to now?" Sam asked. "Another blue Buick with our names on it?"

"Some of the boys in Litigation are being asked, discreetly, about cutting the firm's losses on our Chicago friends," Oscar said. "Perhaps even going to the FBI."

Sam had to gulp. This was a lot. "Who's doing the asking? Cupcake?"

"Who's Cupcake?" Oscar asked.

"Sorry, that's our nickname for Robert. Long story."

"I'm sure the name fits. Yes, he's the one making the inquiries, with all the discretion of a bull moose. About the same level of class you'd expect from a guy who tried to stage a hit and run in Midtown Manhattan," Oscar said.

"He doesn't ever act on his own," Sam said. "Who's putting him up to it?"

"Matriarch Laura, of course." Oscar replied. "Cupcake, as you call him, isn't too good at covering his tracks." Oscar Sampson clearly had many influential friends remaining at Fishbein, Schindler, Rose and Sampson. Just not the Matriarchs.

The car was moving at about 75 miles per hour. Fast, but fairly typical for the interstate between Milwaukee and Chicago. People were always in a hurry. As he was steering along the multiple lanes, leading traffic instead of just keeping pace, smelling his mentor's cigarette, Sam decided to ask the big question.

"Was Peter DeSantis laundering money?"

"Probably," Oscar said, very pointedly NOT indicating whether the client's counsel was involved. Oscar was ready to preempt the question. "Your next question is whether there's any actionable evidence."

"Okay," Sam said, clutching the steering wheel a little more tightly to keep his hands from shaking.

"You met Peter DeSantis on numerous occasions, Sam," Oscar said. "He and I were close. But do you think he told his lawyer everything he did?"

"Peter DeSantis built a business in Chicago starting in the 1950s. He made deals with suspected, though never convicted, mob figures like Tony Addison," Sam said. "No, I don't think he told anyone everything."

"But he did keep records," Oscar said, blowing cigarette smoke out the crack in the window.

"The paper trail we've seen has lots of holes in it," Sam said. "A lot of it was probably shredded and burned." Sam remembered Tony Addison's Shred Sleds, and their motto: *Your business is no one else's business.*

"I'm confident that Peter DeSantis kept a record of all the important transactions," Oscar continued. "All the big deals. Certainly a record of where all the money went, and how much he paid people."

"And those records weren't stored at the Chicago offices of DeSantis Industries, or with his counsel?" Sam asked.

"Of course not," Oscar replied.

"So where are they?"

"I think whatever's left is probably at Peter's personal headquarters," Oscar said.

"His penthouse at the John Hancock Center?" Sam asked.

"Yes. I have an envelope with a key and a swipe card in it," Oscar said, pulling another drag off his Kent. "They open a small file closet in the office. I've never had occasion to use them till now."

"And you'd like me to go take a look?"

"Well, I certainly can't be seen inside the building," Oscar said. "I'd have five nosy reporters up my ass."

Sam laughed. "That's quite an image."

Oscar laughed too. Anything to reduce the rising tension of this conversation.

"How would I get in, snoop around, and not raise suspicions?" Sam asked.

"Well, going in as junior counsel conducting an investigation would certainly make no sense," Oscar said. "But going in as part of a real estate appraisal team to assess the property's current market value would work."

"Going in as part of a team?" Sam asked.

"Yes," Oscar said. "What's that lovely young associate named Sandi doing these days? Wouldn't she welcome an opportunity to get out of that New York snake pit for a little project?"

Sam could only shake his head. "Genius," he said, looking over at a smiling, smoking Oscar Sampson.

Forty-Three

Just as Sam was speeding away from Milwaukee, his big brother was speeding towards it.

Jacob had swabbed his cheek as soon as he returned to his Brooklyn home after the Bryant Park meeting with Jane Chapnick. He filled out the consent form, and noted his cell phone number. He took the package to his local post office, and sent it out Priority Mail.

Then, he packed a bag, gassed up his truck, said a little prayer that the old Ford would survive the trip, and headed west. He knew Theresa's hospital was near Milwaukee, courtesy of the "Law Students Unite to Save Leukemia Victim" story in the *Daily News*. Jacob thought it would make sense to be there if he was a bone marrow match. Either way, he wanted to meet his "real" family. Now was the time to go.

Jacob figured it would take him at least 24 hours to go from the Northeast to the Midwest. He'd moved some, but never traveled. On the map, the path looked like a series of interstate highways, some of them toll roads. He didn't have a lot of money, but didn't think he would need much. He could catch a few winks at a rest stop when he needed to, and pick up fast food when he was hungry. It was what he lived on anyway.

Jacob was born to the same parents as Sam and Theresa, but

his life could not have been more different. They grew up in a comfortable home in a nice suburb, went to good public schools, and had a fairly easy on-ramp to college.

Jacob was the adopted son of two people who should have never gotten married. But they did, and were living in Milwaukee at the time. They wanted a baby boy. Oscar had just told Larry and Barbara Mitcham that they were too young to be parents. After all, they were both still in high school. Give the baby to a family who can care for him, he'd said.

Barbara Mitcham did see Jacob after he was born, though just for a moment. She was groggy from a hard labor, but still could see her husband's eyes in his. An official from the adoption agency was waiting for the baby boy when he was released from the hospital. Oscar Sampson, an aspiring lawyer though still in college, reviewed the short list of documents. So far as he could tell, everything was in order. The biological parents signed. The records were sealed, the baby was spirited away, and Larry and Barbara got back to their lives. Before long they were married, and started their own family. Of course, they never forgot their first son. They just talked about it less and less over the years, and never told Sam and Theresa.

Jacob's adoptive parents didn't stay in Milwaukee for long. They moved around a lot. They fought a lot. They split up a lot. They got back together a lot. They had two more children, but Jacob was the only adopted one.

In spite of the domestic drama, Jacob's adoptive mother was a caring woman, with true affection for her children. While the kids were young, she showered them with attention, and they thrived – especially when their father wasn't around.

Dedicated as she was, Jacob's adoptive mother had some unique views on optimal childrearing. She "didn't believe" in school. Whatever the children needed to know, she could teach them at home. She knew as much as any elementary school teacher, minus the college training, and her children didn't need to be around mean kids on the playground.

It worked when the children were little. It unraveled completely as the children grew into adolescents and adults. They were smart, but never had a real chance to succeed – unless you think of waitressing and flipping burgers as career tracks. Jacob and his adoptive siblings were uneducated, and didn't develop social skills common to everyone else their ages. They didn't socialize with other kids.

The one thing they did have was a dedication to what they knew of their family. They could see that their alternative-thinking mother was trying her best, and their father was mostly absent. Given his abusive tendencies, no one minded his tendency to go missing.

Jacob didn't go to school, but he did learn how to drink. It was a way out, especially when he was around other people who had a chance to develop coping skills. He buried his anger with alcohol; common enough story. Jacob was also unlucky – he got caught a lot. He'd been convicted twice of driving while intoxicated, and knew that a third conviction could mean the end of his license.

He didn't have much in the way of a job either. He was dependable enough, and honest, but had no marketable skills. Certainly nothing like the elite legal training of his little brother. He kept food on the table, and gas in the truck, but just barely.

Jacob learned he was adopted years ago. His adoptive mother told him; she thought he should know. He asked about his biological parents, but there wasn't much for her to tell him. Sealed court records and all that.

Still, it hadn't taken Jane Chapnick that long to find him. The sealed adoption records, opened due to medical emergency, did list the real names of both his biological parents and his adoptive parents. One of Jane's friends was able to make contact with Jacob's adoptive Mom, and she provided Jacob's phone number. They'd lived apart for years, but still talked once in awhile. Whatever anger Jacob felt towards her stayed buried. He sincerely thought she'd done the best she could.

The old Ford pickup was pretty cooperative on the trip west. It started using some oil, but that was it. The interstate system between New York and Wisconsin was fairly functional, as well. The directional signs were clear, the occasional tollways not too overpriced, and many of the rest stops had hamburger stands.

He actually had the most trouble finding the hospital once he was in Wisconsin. Theresa was at a major regional facility just to the west of Milwaukee, but it took a few stops at local gas stations to finally get there.

Driving into the hospital's parking garage, Jacob realized he hadn't showered in two days. He didn't know who would be at the hospital. He'd just come because it felt like the right thing to do. In spite of a few suddenly-emerging second thoughts, he quickly decided that his "real" mother wouldn't care what he looked like. If she was even there.

Jacob entered the hospital's main atrium, and walked past the same rows of wheelchairs that Sam noticed just days before. He approached the information desk, and asked the room number for Theresa Mitcham.

"I'm sorry," the receptionist told him, after checking the computer for patient admissions. "She's in the BMT unit. Immediate family only."

"I am immediate family," Jacob said. "I'm her brother."

"Well, let me just call upstairs and see if we can get you cleared."

The receptionist called the BMT unit. The clerk went into Theresa's room, and asked Mrs. Mitcham if it was okay for her son Jacob to come up.

Barbara Mitcham was waiting for Jacob as he got off the elevator. She had already started crying, and was biting her hand to keep from screaming.

Forty-Four

"How is she?" was the first thing Jacob wanted to know.

"She's been better," his mother said, finally releasing her oldest son from an extended hug.

"How about you?" he asked. Jacob wasn't sure how he was feeling right now, or what he expected to feel after two days on the road and a hospital hallway meeting with his biological mother. Mostly numb.

"I'm okay," she said. "Surprised. I was hoping to meet you, but didn't know it would be so soon."

"I didn't see any sense in waiting," Jacob said.

"We do a lot of waiting around here," Barbara Mitcham said. "Theresa's asleep right now, and sleep is a good thing. Gives her a break."

Jacob laughed at her next line: "Are you hungry?" This was definitely his biological mother.

"Yeah," he said. "And maybe I could get a shower before I meet her?"

"The house is a few miles away. You can clean up, and I can fix you something to eat."

Jacob's arrival would be big news to everyone, and Barbara Mitcham was already trying to figure out who to tell, and when.

The obvious first choice was Theresa. She's the one who needed him most.

But like so many people in times of stress, her first call was to her lawyer. Not her baby-lawyer son, but Oscar Sampson. He was in his luxurious Chicago hotel room, talking by his deskside phone (not a Fish Fone) with a few of his friends at the firm.

"Jacob is here," Barbara said.

"Excuse me?"

"Jacob is here. Actually, he's in the shower. He met with your friend Jane Chapnick, and hopped in the truck. Drove for two days."

"How did he know where to go?" Oscar asked, then immediately said, "Of course, all the news coverage." Oscar was well-acquainted with the sometimes unintended consequences of publicity.

"How is he?" Oscar asked.

"He's dirty and hungry. I'm going to make him something to eat, and then introduce him to his sister," Barbara said, happily placing a kettle on the stove.

Oscar was taken aback that Jacob had jumped the gun, but had ample experience dealing with surprises. He immediately shifted to the next salient issue, as a good lawyer would.

"Did he send in his test?"

"Yes, he told me in the car that he sent it in just before he left, so it should be arriving about now. Is there some way we can expedite that? I know it usually takes up to six weeks to get the test read and listed on the donor directory."

"I will consider that my top priority," Oscar said. *Jane Chapnick could help,* he thought. *Or perhaps one of the health care executives who were so grateful for the generosity of DeSantis Industries.*

"What about Sam?" Barbara asked. "Do you want to tell him he's got a brother, and his brother is in Milwaukee? Or should I call him?"

"He'd jump back in his rental car and drive there tonight,"

Oscar said.

"I know he would. I also know that he's more than a little busy working for you right now."

Oscar paused for a moment. He figured Sam was probably trying to get Sandi to Chicago so they could make their investigative run to the penthouse apartment of Peter DeSantis. Oscar had already finished some of the groundwork to get them into the John Hancock Center, and he didn't want to slow down the mission. Maybe he wouldn't have to.

"My dear, I suggest we take this one step at a time," Oscar said. "Are you sure you're ready for a family reunion with Sam, before Jacob has even met Theresa?"

"Oscar, I don't know what I'm ready for. I almost just burned my hand on the stove. My head is spinning." Barbara Mitcham also felt something approaching pure joy. She thought the break this family needed had now arrived. Literally. And he was in her shower getting ready to meet his little sister, whose life he might be able to save. "It's a lot to take in all at once," she said.

"Here's my suggestion," Oscar said, in the deliberative tone of a veteran counselor. "Why don't you get Jacob fed and go back to the hospital? I'll start work right now on getting the test results. We'll let Sam get a good night's rest."

"Fine with me," Barbara said, and added, "Who could've seen this coming?"

"My thoughts exactly," Oscar said. "But it's wonderful. I'm sure everything will work out just fine."

"Thanks, Oscar. Talk with you soon," she said, hanging up the phone. She had a container of leftover chili in the refrigerator. It would have to do.

Jacob came into the kitchen. He had showered, shaved, and changed into fresh clothes. His biological mother suppressed a gasp. He looked just like Sam, and a lot like Theresa. A little taller, a little thinner, a little older. But from appearances alone, no doubt that he was part of this family.

Jacob tore through two big bowls of chili. He wasn't fussy about food, hadn't eaten anything of substance for two days, and Barbara Mitcham was a good cook. Even her leftovers. The room was filled with the aroma of fine home cooking. It was a smell so familiar to Sam and Theresa that they had almost forgotten it. To Jacob, it was all brand new.

They quickly established that Jacob would be staying for now at her house, at least until they figured out what to do next. Barbara showed him the guest bedroom. She remembered back to the time when her husband Larry argued for this house, over another one in a slightly better neighborhood that had one fewer bedroom. "You never know when you'll need another bedroom," he'd said. "Someday we'll be glad we have it."

Once they got settled, Barbara and Jacob made the five-minute trip back to the hospital and its bone marrow transplant unit. Word had spread not only through the unit, but through a good part of the hospital. Everyone knew about the "Law Students Unite to Save Leukemia Victim" story. And now, a long-lost brother!

All of the nurses on the unit treated Theresa like a favorite little sister, albeit a very ill one. They tried to keep the news from her, but one of them just spilled it as soon as Theresa woke up from her nap. For the first time in weeks, she forgot about her pain and her nausea and her prognosis.

"Hi, Jacob," she said, as soon as they entered the room. She was smiling for the first time in weeks.

"Mom," she said, "you have some explaining to do."

Forty-Five

Sam made the point to Oscar that they could bring Sandi in from New York, without arousing the suspicion of Cupcake or the Matriarchs, by simply conducting the inspection over the weekend. Sam could handle the travel arrangements through the Chicago office, Sandi could stay in touch with Cupcake via Fish Fone, and she'd be back in New York before anyone noticed she was gone. At this point, Oscar very much liked the idea of keeping things simple.

The remaining staff of Peter DeSantis, notably his housekeeper Bernice, was happy to accommodate Oscar's request for access to the John Hancock Center penthouse. After all, she was grateful to remain on his payroll, and the request to bring in a real estate appraisal team made sense. Oscar reassured Bernice that the penthouse wouldn't be sold anytime soon, but that it was necessary to get an up-to-date appraisal.

Sandi was excited at the prospect of doing something other than recruiting law students for the bone marrow registry, and whatever drudge work Cupcake threw at her on a daily basis. She automatically packed a few business suits, as Sam knew she would.

Oscar hadn't brought Sam up-to-date on all the news from Milwaukee. Oscar explained to Barbara that he needed Sam for some weekend business meetings. She had plenty to do in Milwaukee, and was happy to remain cryptic in her phone updates with Sam. He was none the wiser, with plenty to do himself, and the assumption that nothing was happening in Milwaukee beyond the waiting and hoping.

Oscar did tell Sam that Bernice Andrews had been employed by Peter DeSantis for decades, ever since DeSantis became rich enough to afford a full-time housekeeper. Oscar described her as hard-working, conscientious and discreet. She was waiting for Sam and Sandi in the Hancock Center lobby on Saturday morning.

Sam and Sandi did their best to look like real estate appraisers. He wore a suit, she wore a suit. Real estate appraisers look a lot like lawyers. Bernice thought they looked a little young, but if Oscar Sampson sent them, that was enough for her.

On the ride up in the elevator, Bernice joked that the DeSantis penthouse was so high up that it was often literally in the clouds, and if she wanted to know the weather at street level she had to call down to the lobby and ask. Sam and Sandi just looked at each other and smiled. This was a different world from the one they knew.

The penthouse was lovely, and certainly had the best views in Chicago, but it was not as over-the-top as Sam and Sandi expected. It just looked really comfortable. A living / dining / kitchen area, three bedrooms with bathrooms, and a study. Outside of the view, the one nod to true wealth was the private elevator going from the study to the parking garage. Of course, the whole place was spotless. Bernice had been seeing to that for years. She had been the one insisting to Oscar that once the crime scene investigators were out, the blood-stained leather chair in the study had to go. It went.

Along with all the other features in the penthouse, Bernice pointed out the private file closet in the study. It wasn't equipped with an alarm, she said, but was protected by several locks and keys. Thinking Sam and Sandi were real estate appraisers, she explained the file closet would accommodate private papers, and not much more. It wasn't very big. She apologized that she didn't have the necessary keys to show them inside. She assumed those were in Oscar's possession. Actually, at that moment, they were in Sam's pocket.

Sam and Sandi dutifully took notes during their tour, and kept hoping that Bernice would give them a little time alone in the apartment. Not a chance. Bernice was their hostess, and was responsible for this apartment. Even if it was vacant, and its former resident was dead.

Oscar thought Bernice would hover, which is why he advocated sending Sam and Sandi in together. At the appropriate time, Sandi's job would be to distract Bernice. Sam's job would be to check out the file closet.

That time was now, and Sandi knew it. While they were still in the study, Sandi said: "My colleague is a whole lot more interested in this study and the private elevator than I am. Would you mind showing me the kitchen again?"

It worked. "I understand that in real estate, the value of a place comes from the kitchen and bathrooms," Bernice said, leading Sandi back outside the study. Sam stayed in, knowing he'd have just a couple of minutes.

Sam had already looked inside the envelope Oscar had given him. There was just one key and an electronic swipe card. Hoping Bernice was right, and that this private room didn't have an alarm, Sam put the key in the closet door lock, and swiped the card against the magnetic card reader right outside the door. His heart started pumping faster.

The door popped open. A light came from inside, automatically. Sam backed up, to accommodate the door as it swung open. He paused after the light came on, wondering if anything else would happen. It flashed through his mind that he had been trained as a lawyer, not as a private detective. *What if there was an electric eye on this room? Why wouldn't a multimillionaire have intense security on his inner sanctum?*

Oscar had simply shrugged his shoulders to every question, saying "I don't know, Sam. I was Peter DeSantis' good friend, and the lawyer on most things. But I was never under the illusion that he told me everything he did. Nor would I want to take responsibility for everything he did."

None of that was much comfort right now. Oscar was in his swanky hotel room, Sandi was out in the kitchen with the loyal housekeeper, and Sam was the one going into the double-locked closet.

In for a penny, in for a pound, Sam thought to himself. It was one of those inane lines he had heard once from his Mom. He didn't really know what it meant, but it seemed to fit right now. Sam would never admit it out loud, but he wished his Mom was here to hold his hand.

Sam stepped inside. There were no flashing lights, no alarms, no spears shot at him from secret gun turrets inside the closet's walls. After about 10 seconds, he heard Sandi's voice. She was signaling that Bernice was on the way back.

Get out, now, he thought.

Sam stepped out of the room, closed the door, and took out the key. The door locked. He was able to quickly compose himself, and assumed a fake pose next to the window.

"It is quite a view," Sam said as the two women reentered the study. "One of the best I've ever seen in Chicago."

"Yes, it's amazing, isn't it?" Bernice asked. "I've been coming up here for years, and I've never forgotten how special it is."

Bernice then asked the first question on her mind. It was probably the last thing Sam or Sandi was thinking of. "Well, how much do you think it's worth in today's market?"

Sandi was ready to reply. "We have some homework to do back at the office, but I feel pretty confident in saying that this penthouse has appreciated considerably since it was assessed at $15 million. You've certainly maintained it beautifully."

"What about the recent history, may Mr. DeSantis rest in

peace," Bernice said.

Sandi kept going. She was ready for this. Good thing, because Sam was still wobbly. "Well, of course there is the notoriety to consider," she said. "But Mr. Sampson does not intend to offer this property for the foreseeable future, and notoriety does fade over time."

That seemed to satisfy Bernice, who was content to escort the real estate appraisers back to the lobby, and wish them well. She'd be happy to help them out again, anytime. As long as it was arranged through Mr. Sampson, of course.

Sandi waited until they were safely inside the rental car. Sam got in the passenger seat. He was in no shape to drive. Sandi waved at Bernice back in the lobby, started the car, and drove down the street.

"Well?" she said, once they were out of sight of the John Hancock Center.

"There wasn't much in there," Sam said.

"I'm not surprised to hear that. There are big gaps in the DeSantis files, and we always thought that the really sensitive stuff was destroyed."

"No, it's there."

"I'm not following," she said, trying to look at Sam while keeping the car on the road.

"I only had a few seconds, but I could see the closet was mostly bare. There were just three file boxes sitting on a shelf," Sam said

"Did you look inside them?" she asked.

"Nope, didn't have a chance," he replied. "But I could see how they were labeled."

"How?" Sandi asked.

"One said 'Addison Trucking.' The second said 'Restructuring.' The third said 'Private Finances,'" Sam said.

"Wow," Sandi said.

"Wow is right," Sam said. "Let's go back to the airport. You need to return to New York."

"And what are you going to do?"

"It's time for Oscar to tell me the rest of the DeSantis story," Sam said. "Especially why his primary client left behind copies of the files that probably explain everything."

"What do you think?" Sandi asked.

"I think Peter DeSantis knew his lawyer might need those files, and gave him the keys, right before he died," Sam said.

"I'm not following you," Sandi said.

"DeSantis knew he was about to die," Sam said. "Maybe he wanted to die."

They drove in silence until Sandi pulled up to the curb at O'Hare.

"Are you okay?" she asked him.

"Well, other than feeling as though I saw the ghost of Peter DeSantis in that closet, I'm just fine," Sam said.

"I think maybe it *is* time for you to have a talk with Oscar," she said. "He owes you an explanation as to why he put us up to this, and what he expected us to find."

Sam silently reviewed everything that had happened since he began his career at Fishbein. The early promise. The news of Albert Rose's suspicious death. The almost immediate assignment to Oscar Sampson. The labyrinthine DeSantis bankruptcy case. The shooting death of Peter DeSantis. The murder investigation. The Blue Buick Incident. The sacking of Matriarch Sarah. His new role as a private investigator.

If nothing else, Sam thought, *I've been okay with a vastly expanding level of personal risk.*

His next move seemed the riskiest of all. He reached over to Sandi, slid his hand behind her neck, and gently kissed her on the mouth.

Forty-Six

Sandi didn't want to get back on the plane to New York, but she knew Sam was serious. He needed to confront Oscar, and couldn't do that with her in tow. She'd hear the result soon enough. He said he'd be in touch as soon as he could, and she believed him. *And, he kissed me*, she thought. *Was that for real?*

Sandi decided to wait and see if Cupcake asked her anything about her weekend. There was certainly an electronic record that she had been to Chicago and back on Fishbein's dime, but she didn't know how quickly travel receipts were entered into the expense reporting system.

As it turned out, especially on the DeSantis case, everything went to Cupcake almost instantly. This wasn't like the old days, when Oscar could pretty much do whatever he wanted, as long as his clients were happy and the bills were paid. Oscar was on a much tighter leash now.

Fishbein's entire administrative structure reported into Laura Henderson and not anyone else, even if the "anyone else" was Oscar Sampson. Cupcake alerted Laura immediately that Sandi had been to Chicago, and she had Mindy organize a conference call with the other Matriarchs. It took Mindy less than 15 minutes to round up everyone. She also put Cupcake on standby, so of course he just stared at his Fish Fone, hoping it would summon him at this hour of need.

Laura came on the call last. "Is everyone here?" she asked.

"Yes, Carol, Connie and I are on the line," said Mindy. "And we can conference in Robert if and when we need to." Mindy had already updated the other members of the Fishbein diamond ring club about Cupcake's internal investigation.

"So, it appears our good friends at the Midwest office are up to something," Laura began.

"Both Oscar and Sam have been to Milwaukee and back, though that could be connected to the plight of Mitcham's sister." Laura had authorized surveillance of Fishbein's remaining partner, and she wouldn't have to argue its necessity with this group. She hadn't thought to put a tail on Sam, though that might be a prudent next step.

"And today, though Oscar never left his hotel room, Sandi went from New York to Chicago and back again," Mindy said. "I thought she was with us, but it appears not." So much for that nice luncheon and all the fashion tips.

"Has Robert confronted her about going to Chicago without his authorization?" asked Carol. "We could easily fire her for that alone."

"We could, but she's a collateral player at this point," said Laura. "She probably doesn't know much. This is all Oscar, and Sam Mitcham to a lesser extent. If we confront her, she'll go straight to them."

"Unless we cut her off," offered Connie.

Laura cut Connie off. "Sarah tried that with Sam Mitcham, and it didn't do a bit of good. It may have scared him, but it certainly didn't stop him."

Mindy decided to steer Laura gently to the crisis at hand. No use going backwards, especially not right now. "What do we know about our current liability, and Robert's contact with our litigation partners?"

"Get him on the call," Laura said, which Mindy accomplished

with a few keystrokes.

"Robert, thanks for joining us," Laura began, and with no pause said, "Please tell us where we stand."

Cupcake had talked with several litigation partners, in what he assumed was strict confidence. A few of them kept their mouths shut, fearing Laura's ability to make their lives difficult. The older ones immediately called Oscar, so he knew what Cupcake was about to say.

"The litigators say that there is some material risk to the firm, and of course they expressed their deep concern as partners," he began.

"Do they recommend going to the FBI?" Laura said.

"They all noted the apparent absence of physical evidence in the case," he continued.

"Go on," Laura said.

"The historical files on DeSantis, especially going back some years when the real money was made, seem to have been purged," he said. "The litigators say that someone could make a case that Fishbein knew when and how money laundering began, but it would be a tough case to prove. There's also no evidence that Oscar Sampson was personally involved. Peter DeSantis was known as a strong and independent businessman. In Chicago, no less."

"And we're confident all the real evidence has been destroyed?" Laura asked.

"What we know is that nothing of real substance, nothing that could imply concerted criminal activity, has surfaced so far."

"That's not very reassuring," Laura said, "given that Oscar controls all the files in Chicago."

"Well, we have some tidbits here and there, but you're substantially correct." Robert immediately regretted trying to sound like an in-control lawyer, remembering that Laura had only gone as far as becoming a paralegal.

"So Fishbein, Schindler, Rose and Sampson has a dead client, but no smoking gun. Other than the actual murder weapon."

"None that we know of," Cupcake said.

"Damn it, what is Sampson doing in Chicago?" Laura asked. "What haven't we thought of?"

The conference call went mute.

"There's a significant piece of this that's missing," Laura finally said. "I can just feel it. Oscar is staying put in Chicago, almost daring me to come after him."

No input from any other Matriarch.

Laura wasn't actually the first person on Oscar's mind, but he was certainly the first on hers. He was the one remaining obstacle between her and real control of the firm. And she didn't know what he was doing.

Laura knew she had at least one more card to play in this game. She could confront Oscar Sampson in person. He was afraid of her, and she knew it. He thought, for some reason, that Laura and her Matriarchs were trying to kill him.

Forty-Seven

Oscar Sampson believed in protecting his clients and his friends. But protecting didn't mean sugar-coating. Oscar felt more than a little guilty about involving Barbara Mitcham's son in his escalating battle with the Matriarchs.

"They've got surveillance on me," he said to Barbara on the phone.

"How can you tell?" she asked.

"There's a private detective in the hotel lobby," he replied. "Another one in a car outside the hotel. Another one in a van outside the offices of DeSantis Industries."

"Are they watching Sam too?" Barbara asked.

"I wouldn't be surprised," he said.

"So what can you do?"

"Try to lay low," he said. "I've been staying on a regular routine, just going between the hotel and the office."

"How about your phone calls?" she asked.

"I'm talking with you on my personal cell phone," he said. "I don't think Laura has the connections to trace cell phone calls, especially if I keep them short."

"Did you take a risk coming up here to Milwaukee?"

"A small one," he replied. "Laura probably figures that trip was connected to our search for a donor. I went right from the Milwaukee airport to the hospital, and had Sam drive me right back to our Chicago hotel."

"Have you told Sam about Jacob yet?" she asked.

"No, but I will soon," he said. "I just had Sam and Sandi run an errand for me, and I'm waiting for him to report back."

"Is there something going on between those two?" Sam's Mom asked.

"They seem suited to each other, don't they?" Oscar replied.

"Don't tell me you're playing matchmaker again?" she said, with a laugh.

"I did all right with you and Larry, didn't I?" he asked.

"You certainly did," she replied.

Oscar anticipated that Sandi's trip to Chicago for the penthouse visit would be noticed eventually, but he didn't anticipate it getting back to Laura as quickly as it had. Oscar knew a confrontation with her was coming, and he really was afraid of her. First, though, he'd have to deal with Sam.

Sam didn't waste any time. As soon as Sandi had been dropped off at O'Hare, he drove back to the hotel, and was knocking at the door of Oscar's hotel suite. Sam wasn't happy. *Sandi and I were set up by my supposed mentor*, he thought, *and it's time to get to the bottom of it.*

There was a message on his cell phone to call Theresa, but the tone of her voice actually sounded upbeat, so it could wait until Sam got a few answers from Oscar. The laser focus on business was also a way to avoid thinking about his impulsive kiss at the airport curb.

"Bernice says hello," Sam said, walking briskly though the door as soon as Oscar opened it. "She misses seeing you at the penthouse." Sam threw his coat on the couch, sat down, and folded his arms.

"It's quite a place," Oscar said, taking the chair next to Sam.

"With a nice little file closet. No trouble getting inside, once

Sandi distracted Bernice in the kitchen." Sam's face was getting red.

"Bernice has been a dedicated employee for years. I don't think she ever went in that file closet herself. I never did."

"Why didn't the police investigators go in there after DeSantis was found dead?" Sam demanded.

"They didn't ask to. It isn't a wall safe, it's a little file closet. They mostly focused on the immediate area around the body. I suppose it could be argued that once they saw it was a professional hit, they didn't look very hard for other clues."

"But you knew it was there," Sam said. His arms were still folded. His fear had drained away. What he felt now was anger.

"Peter told me he'd be leaving behind some papers in case they were ever needed," Oscar said. "That's honestly all he said on that subject. I never saw them."

"I haven't seen them either. All I had time to do was look at the boxes, labeled 'Addison Trucking,' 'Restructuring,' and 'Personal Finances.'"

"That would about cover it," Oscar said. "You didn't look inside the boxes?"

"I didn't have time to. You knew I wouldn't have time to."

Oscar shifted in his chair, and folded his hands. "I needed to confirm what Peter told me was actually inside the closet," he said. "You did that, with just a glance."

"Though we wouldn't know without actually reviewing the contents, those boxes probably are the only real hurdle to solving the current problems at DeSantis Industries," Sam said.

"It's ironic," Oscar said. "Peter did not intend to leave behind problems."

"Because they're the only records of some of the shadier deals," Sam said. "The money that was made. The money that was paid out. Where the money was stored. Where the money was laundered."

"Right," Oscar admitted.

"And you want me to believe that you didn't know the details of anything that wasn't legal."

"That happens to be the truth," Oscar said. "At most, and I mean at most, I was guilty of looking the other way at a few significant moments in the development of DeSantis Industries. Especially since everything Peter did worked." Oscar wasn't used to being on the receiving end of so many questions.

"Actually, on that score, I believe you," Sam said, remembering the business culture of the 1950's, and all the subsequent profits of DeSantis Industries.

"Thank you, son." Oscar said, knowing they weren't done yet. He paused, folded his hands the other way, then said, "Go on. Ask your next question. It's time you knew the rest."

"Peter DeSantis wanted to die, didn't he?" Sam asked.

"Yes," Oscar began. "More to the point, he knew he was going to die, and soon. Peter believed in maximum control. He wanted to call the shots. Literally."

"He was sick, right?" Sam asked.

"Yes. He called it 'The Fatal Cocktail.' A brain tumor, plus pancreatic cancer."

"And he'd already been to see the best specialists in the world," Sam said.

"Of course," Oscar replied. "Peter had many connections in the health care arena. He funded a lot of research over the years."

"How much time did they give him?" Sam asked.

"A month or less," Oscar said. "It was clear the pain would get much worse, and Peter did not like pain."

"Hence the three-martini lunches," Sam said.

"Peter was drinking a lot towards the end," Oscar said. "Not just at lunch. Who could blame him?"

Sam paused for a moment, remembering the gregarious, bright, and funny Peter DeSantis he met at those power restaurant lunches. *So many secrets buried, and Peter DeSantis intended to keep them buried,* Sam thought.

"Did you know in advance how it would work?" Sam asked, his tone quieter now.

"We talked about it briefly," Oscar said. "He gave me the keys to the file closet, and told me to stay away unless I really needed the information."

"He arranged for someone to come up and shoot him at close range? How could he possibly do that?" Sam asked.

"I asked him the same thing," Oscar replied. "The final deal he made with Tony Addison involved one more step."

"One more step?"

"Yes," Oscar said. "Addison's man came up in the private elevator at the appointed hour, just as DeSantis was making some phone calls to inquire about Theresa's care."

"I remember the phone log," Sam said.

"So that established the time line for whatever light investigation would follow," Oscar said.

"Okay, then what?"

"Addison's guy knew how to administer an injection," Oscar said.

"DeSantis was unconscious when he was shot?"

"Exactly," Oscar said. "You've heard of Propofol, the drug Michael Jackson died from?"

"Yeah, I remember the news reports," Sam said.

"Propofol is a powerful IV medication they use in emergency rooms to knock people out quickly," Oscar said. "Peter DeSantis calculated, correctly, that no one would look for a small needle mark on a man who had taken obviously fatal shots to the head."

"That is one wicked calculation," Sam said.

"Knowing him, he probably took real pleasure in controlling not only the mechanics of his death, but how it would be perceived afterwards."

"It was a hell of a way to go out," Sam said.

"He figured a criminal investigation would go nowhere, and

buy some time for me to salvage his company and protect his people," Oscar said. "With the files in the closet if I needed them."

"But in terms of criminal liability, not to mention your own tenuous position within the firm, that paper is now a significant hurdle," Sam said. "Laura would use it against you if she knew about it."

"That's exactly what I think," Oscar said.

The two lawyers sat silent for a time, just looking at each other, making calculations of their own.

Finally, Sam said, "Okay, anything else?" He couldn't imagine that there would be.

"Well, yes, one more thing, but not related to the DeSantis case," Oscar began.

"What?" Sam asked.

"There's quite a bit of news from the bone marrow transplant unit in Milwaukee. I can bring you up to date, or you could return your sister's call."

Forty-Eight

A Wisconsin State Patrolman pulled Sam over for speeding a mile away from the hospital. Sam decided to tell the officer about half of his story, and said he was hurrying to the bone marrow transplant unit to meet his just-discovered brother, who might be able to save his sister's life.

The veteran cop knew the truth when he heard it, and let Sam go.

Sam quickly drove to the hospital's parking lot, so overwhelmed by what he'd just heard from Oscar, and what was waiting upstairs, that he didn't see the private detective in the lobby. Even though Oscar had told him to keep an eye out.

Jacob quickly extended his hand to Sam, in the manner of Midwestern men who always shake hands but don't hug.

"Hi, I'm Jacob."

"Sam."

"I'm not a match either," Jacob said.

"Excuse me?" Sam asked.

"We just got a call from someone named Oscar Sampson," Jacob said. "I'm not a match."

Sam quickly glanced at his sister, who seemed as stunned as he was. He stumbled over to his Mom, gave her a hug, and waited for an explanation.

"Oscar just phoned from Chicago," Barbara Mitcham told the room, repeating what was obviously very fresh news for everyone.

"And you're not a match," Sam said, looking at the taller brother he was meeting for the first time. *I've gotta give Oscar credit for multi-tasking,* Sam thought.

"No," said Jacob. "But we knew the odds were about 25 percent. Just like you. Same biological parents and all."

Sam looked over at his very ill sister. She was smiling. *Smiling?* Barbara Mitcham started to smile too.

Jacob looked a little perplexed; he didn't know everyone yet.

"But there is a match," Theresa said.

"What?" Sam asked.

"Oscar said that there's a perfect ten-for-ten match," Theresa said. "From one of the people you guys recruited into the bone marrow registry."

"You're kidding," Sam said.

"Nope, swear to God," Theresa said. "A ten-for-ten match. She probably has all the same allergies I do."

"Who?" Sam asked.

"Wanna guess?" his sister asked, with the first thing she had to be playful about in months. "You know her pretty well."

"No shit?" Sam said, knowing his Mom wouldn't call him on his salty language this time.

"Yeah," Theresa said. "Sandi."

"That whole donor recruiting effort was her idea," Sam said. "Not to mention all the legwork in New York." *Not to mention I kissed her,* he thought.

"I know. Kind of perfect, isn't it?" Theresa asked. "And we meet Jacob as a bonus."

Sam looked over at his big brother. Jacob looked a little baffled, yet seemed to understand that Theresa's match had been found, and was someone they already knew. "What are the odds?" Jacob said, shrugging his shoulders.

"Astronomically against," Sam said. *Just like everything else.*

"Well, things happen for a reason." Barbara Mitcham said. "And Oscar said this isn't the only thing coming to a head today. There's news from Chicago?"

It was time for Sam to sit down. "I don't know where to begin," he said.

Jacob and Barbara sat down in the two available chairs, forming a semi-circle around Theresa's hospital bed.

"We already told Jacob some of the basics," Theresa said, trying to be helpful.

"I know you work for a big law firm, and a couple of people are dead," Jacob said. "Albert Rose and Peter DeSantis."

"Well, that's blunt," Sam said. *But true.*

Barbara knew more than anyone in this circle besides Sam, and since he was too overwhelmed to share the full story right now, she began filling in the blanks for Jacob. And asking questions. "Oscar's biggest client was Peter DeSantis. He was found dead. Everyone said it was a professional job. Sam, does Oscar know who killed him?"

"Yes, he does," Sam said. "But then, he always did."

"Oscar is responsible?" his Mom asked.

"No, not directly," Sam said. "DeSantis was sick. Terminal. Brain tumor and pancreatic cancer. He didn't have much time, and his business was a mess."

"I'm not following you," their Mom said.

"Peter DeSantis ordered a hit on himself," Sam said.

"I know what it's like to feel so sick you want to die," Theresa said, prompting her Mom and two brothers to simultaneously nod in her direction.

"And Oscar Sampson helped?" Jacob asked.

"That's pretty much it," Sam said.

"And this lawyer is the guy you've known since high school?" Jacob asked, turning to his biological mother.

"Yes. Actually, he helped arrange your adoption, before he went to law school," Barbara said. "More recently, he's become Sam's boss, and has helped a lot with Theresa's care."

"And he's the guy battling these women you've been telling me about," Jacob said. "What're they called?"

"Everyone calls them the Matriarchs," Barbara said. "They pretty much control the law firm. I know that type of woman."

"That type of woman?" Sam asked.

"The type who break men down, bit by bit, all three of those partners over the course of many years," his Mom said. "Now they're targeting Oscar."

Jacob, having been mostly on the defendant side of the law, knew what to ask next.

"Have they got evidence linking your friend Oscar to the death, and the money laundering?"

Sam looked at Jacob, then at his Mom and sister. "Money laundering?" Sam asked. *Did they use any discretion at all when bringing Jacob up to date?* He decided to bite his tongue on that one.

"Well?" Barbara Mitcham asked her youngest son. "What have they got?"

"DeSantis left behind three boxes of records in his Chicago penthouse," Sam said, turning to Theresa. "Your future bone marrow donor and I tried to check them out, but I only had time to see the boxes sitting there. I didn't get to look inside at the actual files."

"How did you get in the penthouse?" Jacob asked.

"Oscar made up a story about us being real estate appraisers," Sam said. "He gave me two keys to open the file closet. Sandi distracted the housekeeper, I opened the door, and got a quick look before they came back."

"Those boxes of files are the only evidence?" Barbara asked

her son. "And Oscar hasn't seen them?"

"I don't think so," Sam said. "Everything else was shredded a long time ago. That's the way Peter DeSantis ran his business."

"And even if there's not a court case, those files could be used against Oscar by the Matriarchs?" she said, continuing her perceptive line of questioning.

"Probably," Sam said. "They're playing for keeps. They want him out. Probably me and Sandi too, once they take care of him."

"Did Oscar ask you to return the keys to him?" his Mom asked.

Sam hadn't thought of that. "No," he said. "They're still in my pocket."

Barbara Mitcham put her hand over her mouth for a moment, not to suppress any words but to encourage silence while she thought a few steps ahead for the entire family. It didn't take her long.

"Well, everyone," she began. "I know we've already dealt with a lot today. But, I don't think we're done yet. It's time for this family to do Oscar Sampson a favor. God knows we owe him."

I think it's mutual, Sam thought, again biting his lip.

Jacob just started nodding, then looked towards Sam.

"I'm not sure about those women you work with," Jacob said, "but it looks to me as though the real Matriarch is right here." Barbara Mitcham nodded in the direction of her new son to acknowledge his compliment.

"This won't be without risk," she said. "Oscar is now under surveillance, and there's probably someone keeping an eye on us too."

"But they don't know who I am," Jacob said. "How hard could it be for me to get out of here? I could just wear a baseball cap low over my forehead."

Forty-Nine

Technically, Sam did NOT give the penthouse file closet keys to Jacob. Sensing hesitation on the part of the lawyer in the family, Jacob simply took them out of Sam's pocket.

"Tell me what you know about the security system," Jacob said.

"Next to nothing," Sam said. "The housekeeper, a woman named Bernice, let us in and took us up."

"But you said there's a private elevator that goes up from the parking garage," Jacob said. "It was probably used by whoever did the hit on DeSantis. And there's no camera in the elevator."

"That's what the police report said," Sam replied.

"Are there cameras going into the garage?" Jacob asked.

"I don't think so. But there's probably a guard or an ID card swipe system or something."

"Okay, I should be able to get past that," Jacob said.

"That would probably be trespassing," Sam said, with a bit of authority in his voice.

"I thought you specialized in corporate law, with a few months' experience in children's court." Jacob had learned a lot, very quickly. He was a Mitcham, and that meant smart. And fast.

"Fair point," Sam said. "You seem to know more about

criminal law than I do."

"That's enough," Barbara Mitcham interjected, realizing she had just broken up the first fight between her two sons. "I think it's worth a trip to Chicago, if Jacob is willing to go."

"So do I," Theresa said, from her hospital bed.

Sam stopped talking. He didn't really object to Jacob's mission either. *I performed my lawyer role, which was to point out the obvious risk,* he thought. Sam had already gathered enough about Jacob's history to know such risks were a standard part of his brother's life. It was a very different history than the one he'd had.

Getting past the detective in the lobby was a breeze. The subject of surveillance was Sam, not a taller guy with a navy blue New York Yankees baseball cap.

Back in New York, Cupcake was closely monitoring Sam's Fish Fone, but had no access to Sam's personal cell phone, so Sam was able to provide directions to Jacob from the hospital to the Interstate, south for an hour or so, then downtown to the John Hancock Center. From there on, Jacob would be on his own while Barbara, Theresa, and Sam Mitcham waited.

The next part seemed too easy. Jacob was dressed like a maintenance man, and he was driving a pickup truck, so his plan was to approach the guard at the entrance to the parking garage, and see if he could just talk his way in. But, he didn't have to. There was no guard, just a gate that was already open.

"I'm going in," Jacob said on the cell phone.

"Be careful," Barbara Mitcham replied to her son.

Another easy maneuver followed. There was a parking spot right next to the elevator with the *Penthouse. No Admittance,* sign on the door. Jacob went in, and pressed the *P* button on the panel. The car started moving up, quickly. Lots of floors zipped by.

On the ride up, Jacob started to worry about the next part of this operation, which he had not thought through. As the elevator door opened into the penthouse, he realized that if anyone was actually up there, the best he could do was play the part of a maintenance man who got lost, or at worst stepped into the wrong elevator.

Someone was waiting for him. Not in the big new leather chair behind the big executive desk, but in one of the smaller chairs in front of the desk.

"Who are you?" the woman asked him.

"My name is Jacob," he said. *Why make up a name at a time like this?* he thought.

"I'm Bernice," she said. "The housekeeper. Did Oscar send you up?"

"No, I'm here to fix the radiator," Jacob said. It was the first thing that popped into his head. He actually had fixed a few radiators back in New York.

"Nice try, kid. No radiators on this floor. Or anywhere in the building."

Jacob just looked at the Chicago housekeeper for a moment. She was working class, just like him. Probably street smart, just like him.

"You look just like that phony real estate appraiser Oscar sent up here," Bernice said. "He went sniffing around the double-locked file closet. Is that what you're here for too? You got keys?"

Jacob had gotten by a detective in a hospital waiting room. No such luck with Bernice. Jacob was willing to lie, but did a quick calculation that it wouldn't do any good. *I don't have a convincing lie for this occasion,* he thought. *Better to go with the truth.*

"We're trying to help Oscar," Jacob said. "He did send in my little brother, but he doesn't know I'm here. I haven't even met him."

"Have you got keys?" Bernice said again.

"Yes," Jacob said. "But I don't know how they work."

"Okay, I believe you," Bernice said. "You certainly don't look like a professional to me."

"Thanks, I think," Jacob said.

"What do you need?" Bernice asked.

"Sam ... my little brother ... saw three boxes in the file closet," Jacob said. "They probably contain evidence."

"Evidence of what?" Bernice asked. "A murder? I don't think there was a murder. And I'll bet Oscar Sampson knows that too."

"Yeah, I heard the story," Jacob said. "But isn't there a lot more to this? My little brother thinks the boxes contain records of all the old business deals."

"So why wouldn't the lawyer, Oscar, have copies?" Bernice asked.

Jacob was starting to like Bernice. *She's a straight shooter*, he thought, *just like me.*

"I'm the wrong guy to ask. I'm just running the errand," Jacob said. "Oscar is in some big fight with the women who run his law firm, and those papers could sink him."

"So you want to take the boxes out, destroy the records, and just tell Oscar they're gone?' Bernice asked.

"That's about as much of a plan as we've got," Jacob admitted.

Bernice thought for a long minute. Then, looking directly at Jacob, she said, "I have been cleaning up this place for the past 20 years. I guess one more time isn't going to hurt. Open the door."

With more time to match the keys into the slots than his brother had the last time, Jacob opened the closet door. The light popped on, just as it had when Sam grabbed a look. Inside, the little room was empty, except for the three boxes.

"Do you just want to take them out, or should we look inside?" Bernice asked. Her curiosity had been building during the investigation, but she was never in a position to say anything. *I certainly wouldn't cross the lawyer who had been so nice to me before and was keeping me on the payroll now,* she thought. She figured Oscar knew what she knew, and lots more.

"Let's look," said Jacob, grabbing the first box. It was marked "Addison Trucking," and was very light to the touch. He removed the cover. Empty.

"What the hell?" Bernice said.

Jacob was thinking the same thing.

The second box, marked 'Restructuring," also sprang lightly into Jacob's hand. It, too, was empty.

Neither Jacob nor Bernice now expected to see anything in the third, marked "Personal Finances."

Empty, empty, empty! All three!

"I don't get it," Jacob said, tossing the boxes against the file closet wall.

"I think I do," Bernice said, with a sigh.

"I'm all ears," Jacob said.

"Peter DeSantis liked to be in control. Of this penthouse. Of his company. Of his employees. Hell, I think he even controlled his own death."

"Yeah, so why the empty boxes, when he told Oscar there was something in them?" Jacob asked.

"Because he also controlled his lawyer, by never telling him everything. He wanted Oscar to clean up his messes after he was gone, not add to the mess himself."

"He knew Oscar would send someone up to check on the boxes?"

"Sure, why not?" Bernice replied. "He knew I'd never give anyone more than a glance inside."

"You do run a tight ship," Jacob said, with a little admiration.

"I kept the place clean while those two made money," Bernice said. "Call me 'Old School,' but that's what women like me do for men like Oscar Sampson and Peter DeSantis."

"I can see that," Jacob said.

"I'm a paid friend, but I'm still a friend," she added.

Bernice picked up the phone on the desk of Peter DeSantis, and pressed the speed dial button marked *Oscar Sampson*.

Fifty

"Sam, go back to Chicago," Barbara Mitcham said. "Oscar is going to need you."

"What about Jacob, and Theresa, and you?" Sam asked.

"We'll relay any news to you as soon as we have it," his Mom said.

"One more thing, Sam," Theresa said. "You'll have an hour of relative privacy on the way down to Chicago. Don't you want to call my bone marrow donor?"

"I look forward to meeting her soon," Sam's Mom said, with a smile.

"Sandi and I could be looking for jobs soon," Sam said, staring blankly outside the window of Theresa's hospital room. *And they don't even know that I could've met my end with a blue Buick*, he thought.

"Go," Barbara Mitcham instructed. "We'll roll with it, just like we have with everything else over the past two years. Have a little faith."

"More than a little," Sam said.

"More than a little," Theresa agreed.

Sam reluctantly hugged his Mom goodbye. He wasn't allowed to touch his sister because of the continuing infection risk. "At least we have a good shot at making you better," he said to Theresa.

"I think we've got a pretty good shot at making everything better," his sister replied.

On the way out of the building, he noticed the detective in the lobby. Sam walked slowly, just to make sure he was seen, and his trip back to Chicago was relayed to Cupcake and the Matriarchs.

Sam called Sandi on his cell phone as soon as he got on the freeway.

"Hey, pretty lady," he began. "Not to mention, perfect donor."

"Yeah, I guess that's the one bit of good news we have right now," Sandi said.

"It's great news," he said. "What else is going on in New York?"

"Well, Cupcake knows about my trip to Chicago," she said. "He said it was a serious transgression, and that there would be serious consequences."

"Ouch," Sam said.

"The Matriarchs are going to fire me, Sam," Sandi said.

"Not if I can help it," Sam said, noticing on the rental car's instrument panel that he was speeding again. "Not if Oscar can help it, either."

"I don't like other people being in control of my life," Sandi said.

"Me neither," Sam replied. "That's why we became lawyers."

Sam filled Sandi in on the current evidence of his lack of control, namely Oscar's orchestration of Jacob's appearance, aided by Jane Chapnick, and his Mom's engineering of Jacob's trip to Chicago.

"Your Mom, Oscar Sampson, Professor Chapnick," Sandi said. "Thank God they're on our side."

"I'd put them up against the Matriarchs any day," Sam said.

"Any day is probably today," Sandi said. "Laura left New

York this morning. She should be in Chicago by now."

"And Chicago is where I'm heading," Sam said. "I hope Oscar lets me in the room for this."

Fifty-One

Laura Henderson had booked a special hotel conference room for her confrontation with Oscar. They hadn't been in the same room since Laura assigned Sam to Oscar's care. Or Oscar to Sam's care. *Either way, it hasn't worked out as I planned,* she thought. And waited.

Oscar, wearing his best silk suit for the occasion, was stopped on his way into the room by the sight of Sam running down the hallway towards him.

"Hello, Sam," Oscar said, then added, with a grin, "Bernice sends her regards."

"It was Mom's idea to send Jacob to the penthouse," Sam said, panting, and wanting to avoid any potential blame.

"Well, that just goes to show you," Oscar said.

"Goes to show you what?" Sam asked.

"It worked," Oscar said.

"What worked?" Sam asked.

Oscar sat down in one of the plush sofas lining the hallway in the hotel's suite of conference rooms. He motioned for Sam to take a seat beside him.

"Listen carefully, Sam," the senior counsel said.

Sam, who had just run a 50-yard dash to catch Oscar before he headed into the conference room, tried to will his pulse rate to drop. He shuffled a little on the sofa while Oscar waited for him to settle down.

"Women rule the world," Oscar finally said. "The trick for guys like us is to figure out which women to follow. And help them lead. That's as much control as we get. Or need."

"You lost me," Sam said, staring straight into his mentor's eyes.

"There's nothing wrong with the Matriarch model," Oscar said.

"I see plenty wrong," Sam protested.

"You just have to find the right Matriarch," Oscar said. "You were lucky enough to be born with one. It took me a lot longer."

"Okay, whatever," Sam said, passing on Oscar's hard-learned truth in favor of the day's distracting drama. "What did Bernice say?"

"The boxes were empty," Oscar said.

"Empty?" Sam asked.

"Empty," Oscar replied. "Peter DeSantis, God love him, did not leave behind a problem."

"Empty?" Sam asked again.

"No files," Oscar said. "Only one smoking gun, the one Peter intended."

"You lost me again," Sam said.

"I knew Peter DeSantis for decades," Oscar said. "He was my client first, my friend second. He always wanted to be in control of everything, including his lawyer."

"Even from the grave," Sam said.

"Even from the grave," Oscar agreed, nodding his head. "Peter didn't think much of The Rule of Law, and certainly didn't believe in Rule by Lawyers."

"It was always his show," Sam said.

"Yes, but now it's his lawyer's turn," Oscar said. "I'm about to meet with Laura, if you'll excuse me."

"Can I go with you?" Sam asked. *I deserve to see this*, he thought.

"No, not this time," Oscar said. "I'm not going to wipe her face in it. We need her to be Fishbein's First Matriarch in New York. She needs us to clean up and run DeSantis Industries in Chicago."

"That's what the textbooks call 'Win, Win,'" Sam said, starting to get it.

"Want to hear the original rationale for the Matriarchs?" Oscar said, not minding the prospect of keeping Laura waiting for him.

"Absolutely," Sam replied.

"We just copied the social structure of lions and tigers -- the 'pride.' It's the females, my partner Morris Fishbein argued, who actually run the pack."

"But we're a different species," Sam said.

"And we're lawyers," Oscar said. "Think about it. Matriarchs can be nurturing, but willing and able to make tough decisions – even leading the kill – when the fate of the pack is threatened."

"Or just when the pack is hungry," Sam added.

"Morris Fishbein, David Schindler, Albert Rose, and I were already used to being called 'bottom feeders' and 'sharks' by our competitors, newspaper reporters, and even our early clients," Oscar said.

"Your early road was tough," Sam agreed.

"Bottom-feeding sharks could appreciate the novelty, not to mention the brilliance, of anointing a tough 'lions and tigers matriarchy' to run their growing firm," Oscar said.

"And, nobody else noticed," Sam added, amazed.

"Women rule the world," Oscar said again. "Just pick the right ones to follow, do what you can to help, and get out of their way."

Sam didn't have anything else to say. The protégé had learned the master's lesson. He simply smiled, and reached out his hand for Oscar to shake.

"Go get her," Sam said.

"I won't be long," Oscar said, leaving Sam in the hallway. "Let's have a few martinis later. We need to talk about that lovely Sandi."

Fifty-Two

Prior to the call from Bernice, Oscar had been prepared to walk into the sumptuous conference room and cut a deal with Laura that would include his retirement. The terms Oscar would offer had changed.

Oscar Sampson was the best deal lawyer anyone had ever seen, and knew to take advantage when it presented itself. In the lingo of his peers, he was now ready to "Bet the Company."

Laura was at the window of the conference room, wearing her best beige Armani, looking out at the expansive Chicago suburbs. It reminded her that she really felt more comfortable in New York than she ever would in the Midwest. She hoped to be on a flight back very soon.

Laura Henderson did not have Oscar Sampson's legal education, her name on the door of the firm, or the millions of dollars he had pocketed. She had the good fortune to have been noticed by Morris Fishbein for her obvious talent. He trained her, and put her on solid footing to run the business of his firm – before anyone else in the legal profession trusted a woman to do anything but type. And, no one ran the business better than Laura and her Matriarchs. They had proven themselves over and over.

"Laura, it's been a long time," Oscar said, offering her his hand as he entered the room. She shook it.

"Hello, Oscar," she said.

Laura thought she finally had the upper hand over Oscar, and that she would soon be rid of the final named partner. But, something had changed. She could tell from the smile on his face that he was not here to capitulate. Or suggest terms of his retirement for her consideration and presentation to the firm's partnership, as she had hoped.

"I have a bit of news," he began, easing himself into one of the plush conference room chairs. "I know you've been concerned about criminal liability associated with the DeSantis case. We've completed our review of the available records. There is no liability problem."

"Meaning what?" she asked, sitting down herself.

No small talk was going to happen between these two. They were here to cut a deal.

"Meaning we can now proceed to the restructuring of DeSantis Industries," Oscar said. "On favorable terms. Keeping the business intact. Keeping people employed." *Keeping the Matriarchs in charge,* Oscar thought. *Don't you get it?*

"That's a very different assessment than we feared," Laura said.

"Yes, I know," he said. "Of course it will take some time to dispel all the rumors, but I'm now confident we can move to put this behind us."

Laura suddenly appeared ashen. She didn't know the details, but knew Oscar had gotten lucky. She'd lost her leverage. He was staying in.

There was a long pause in the conference room as the two leaders of Fishbein, Schindler, Rose and Sampson looked at each other. Oscar reached for one of the glasses of pre-poured iced tea on the conference table, and took a sip.

"May I continue?" Oscar asked, looking at the woman some thought was responsible for the deaths of one or more of his partners.

"Please do," she said.

"I want to apologize for the unpleasantness between us," he said.

"Excuse me?"

"I mean it," Oscar said, meaning it. "This experience in Chicago, trying to figure out how to save my client, has been a real education in how difficult it is to run a multinational business. You do it brilliantly. You always have. You and your team."

Laura looked blankly at Oscar. *He's complimenting me?* she thought.

"Peter DeSantis took great risks and made a great deal of money," Oscar said. "I sometimes looked the other way on the shoddier deals, as long as he continued winning. But he came very close to running his business into the ground"

"He was murdered," Laura said.

"Let me just say that his death is unlikely to result in a criminal prosecution," Oscar said. "You'll have to trust me on that one."

"Do I have a choice?" Laura asked.

"No, you do not."

Another pause. Hadn't Oscar just been complimenting her? Actually, he was. *The point about the "murder" of DeSantis had to be made to the woman running the firm,* he thought, *and there was no easy way to cover that territory.* Besides, Laura Henderson was not someone Oscar Sampson was used to being nice to.

"I don't think you were involved in the death of Albert Rose," Oscar said, bluntly shifting to the other awkward topic. *Time to clear the air*, he thought.

"No, I wasn't," Laura said. *Now what?* she thought. *Stay on your game.*

"All of my partners essentially worked themselves to death," he admitted.

"Our founding partners, with the possible exception of you, were all classic Type A's," Laura said, thinking of Oscar's many expensed three-martini lunches. "Why would I try to hasten anyone's exit?"

"Ethics aside, it would simply add too much risk," Oscar said. "I hope to avoid their example in my last chapter."

Laura could sense there was more coming from this renowned deal lawyer.

"I do have a few requests, which I hope you'll favorably consider," Oscar began again. This was tougher than the usual deal negotiation. There were some things he wanted, but he also wanted to empower First Matriarch Laura. The fighting through surrogates like Sam and Cupcake was over.

"What can I do?" she asked, feeling as tentative as a woman facing a new landscape should.

"I'd like to stay here in Chicago. There will be a lot of work getting DeSantis Industries back on its feet."

"Of course," Laura said.

"And, I'd like Sam Mitcham to take day-to-day leadership of the team, under my supervision. Robert, or Cupcake as he's now known, has become a liability."

Oscar didn't have to mention the Blue Buick Incident. Laura knew that he knew. Oscar knew Sarah approved the plan, and Sarah was gone. Robert executed the plan, badly, and Robert needed to go too.

"Agreed," Laura said. "Robert is done."

"One more thing," Oscar said.

"Yes?" Laura asked.

"Along with Sam, I'd like Sandi to be reassigned to our Chicago office. I think both of them are more suited to the Midwest than they are to the East Coast." *Not to mention easier access to a bone marrow transplant unit in Milwaukee, where they both need to spend some time*, he thought. *And maybe get to know each other a little better.*

"Agreed," she said.

And that was it. The deal was done. No legal documents required.

They would never be personal friends, but they could be friendly. Oscar again offered his hand. Laura shook it.

She kept waiting for him to add something else. He had just one more thing.

"Until now, I never understood the brilliance of those blue diamonds," he said, gesturing to Laura's ring. "Morris Fishbein was right. They suit you, as much as my silk suits suit me."

Laura allowed a small smile in Oscar's direction as she looked down at her brilliant pale blue diamond. She had two more in her top drawer back at New York headquarters, and could now recruit the right women to wear them.

Oscar remembered Sam's assessment: *Win, Win.* He did. She did. They did.

Laura Henderson stood up, nodded at her remaining founding partner, and left the room. Within a few minutes, she would be on a conference call, updating her Matriarchs.

About the Author

J.D. Fox worked for six years as Director of Communications at Columbia Law School in New York City. From there, he went to one of world's largest corporate law firms.

His sister-in-law, who survived breast cancer and leukemia secondary to breast cancer, had a successful bone marrow transplant at Froedtert & Medical College of Wisconsin.

Mr. Fox donates net proceeds from the sale of this book's first edition to the growing international registries of bone marrow donors.

www.ingramcontent.com/pod-product-compliance
Lightning Source LLC
Chambersburg PA
CBHW071400170526
45165CB00001B/128